Rufai Oseni

Veritas:

The Tale of a Sleeping Giant

herein, the author assumes no responsibility for any errors or omissions. No liability is assumed for damages that may result from the use of information contained within.

First Edition

Printed in Nigeria

If you are out to describe the truth, leave elegance to the tailor.

-   Albert Einstein

Table of Contents

Vanguard of Revolutions

Of coups and Riots

Journey to Infrastructure

The Economy and Corruption Hegemony

Lessons from Singapore

Way Forward

Dedication

To the lineage of every Nigerian, whose blood washes our green fields.

May their blood never be in vain.

Introduction

I never did give anybody hell.
I just told the truth and they thought it was hell.
- Sir Harry Truman

It was Napoleon Bonaparte who predicted, "China is a sleeping giant...when she wakes, she will shake the world."
Alas! In the year 1979, China finally woke up and now, not only is it shaking the world, it has taken the world by storm.
The question on my mind is: When will Nigeria wake up?????

When a person sleeps, there is great dynamism in the interregnum. There is strong possibility that he wakes up to restart his system that erstwhile has been in respite and at rest. Once awake, his strength is rekindled, and like a ram that has charged backwards with its hoofs, he is freshly energized and reinvigorated, ready to confront any assailant. But when someone sleeps indefinitely, fear grips those around, whispering to their ears that the sleeper has gone comatose or probably the extreme, died.

Honestly, my fear and trepidation for the nation called Nigeria is great. And I keep wondering, is Nigeria comatose or is she dead? This fear drove my attempt to in this book, revisit history and at the same time, explore possible means to right the wrongs that bedevil this great country. In deep retrospect, I (and surely, numerous well-meaning Nigerians) find it hard, to unravel why we are so poor in the presence of huge resources and potentials. Frighteningly, the festering decadence from the past and new dynamics of the now, are not only growing more potent with every passing moment, they acutely threaten to snuff life out of her.

In the 1970s, an average Nigerian had more money in his pocket, both in perception and actual cash. I say perception, because economists constantly affirm the role perceptions play in economic disposition. The poverty rate was low, as less than 50 per cent of Nigeria lived in poverty. The Yom Kippur war brought so much wealth, that then Head of State, General Yakubu Gowon had to declare, "Money is not Nigeria's problem but how to spend it." The poverty numbers were pegged at about 19 million. A lot of cash sloshed around, we had the cement armada - the highest amount of cement in the world was imported in Nigeria - piled up at the ports for implementation of various projects. Twenty million tonnes of cement (enough to build an entire city from scratch) was waiting to unload in Lagos. In the 70s, Nigeria had imported more bottles of champagne than any nation in the world until it was sapped away by SAP (Structural Adjustment Programme).

A close friend once told me that in the 70s, with N200, he could comfortably eke out a living in England. But now the case is different, over 70 million Nigerians live in abject poverty. A child entering the education systems of an OECD country has an 80 per cent likelihood of going on to university or some other form of tertiary education; only 6 per cent in sub-Saharan Africa have similar chances.
The ratio of teaching staff to students is 1 − 122 at the University of Abuja and 1 − 144 at the Lagos State University; but the same ratio is 1 − 4 at Harvard University, 1 − 9 at the Massachusetts Institute of Technology (MIT), 1 − 3 at the University of Cambridge, and 1 − 10 at the National University of Singapore.
China's poverty index in the 80s was higher than that of Nigeria's. Twenty five years down the line, reverse is the case as 500 million Chinese have significantly surmounted the poverty hurdle, whilst we have increased the numbers. The refineries do not work. With a combined production capacity of 500,000 barrels across the three refineries in Port Harcourt, Kaduna and Warri, Nigeria still imports Premium Motor Spirit (PMS/petrol). Yet, if the refineries ran optimally, Nigeria is supposed to have 70 million litres of petrol daily. This is more than enough to meet our 40 million litres daily consumption, but corruption has thoroughly destroyed the fabric of our existence. It has become a clandestine needle needling Nigeria.

As at independence, Nigeria's GDP was almost twice that of India's and three times that of China. Today, China has four times Nigeria's GDP per capita and India is almost twice. This is why we need to move away from the mindset of small things - the "god of small things" as Arundhati Roy puts it. It is distressing that our economic and industrial production capacity, which used to be 10% in the 1990s, is now less than 4%. There is copious correlation between the insurgency in the North and the close of textile factories.

In the telecommunications sector, it is reported that the top three states of Lagos, Ogun and Oyo in sum recorded 26.10 per cent of the total voice subscriptions nation-wide. The report said Lagos led in telecommunication usage with 20.39 million active voice subscriptions and 20.12 million GSM users by the end of the third quarter, totalling 14.58 per cent of the total nationwide subscriptions. There is some amount of comfort to be derived here. The recent (less than two decades) evolution in its broader umbrella sector - Information, Communications and Technology (ICT) - is substantially revolutionizing and bringing innovation to the way business is being done through proliferation of young, dynamic, and versatile entrepreneurs. Admittedly, we still have a lot of catching up to do with the rest of the world.

While all these play out, leadership remains a strong, cogent factor, and as Max Siollun stated in his epoch piece on the military's incursion into Nigerian polity, *Soldiers of Fortune*, the transfers of power from one military regime to another were not random.
In his words, "each coup and military government had substantial continuity of personnel. Sadly, these same people have controlled Nigerian political and military life since 1966. Between 1966 and 1979, Nigerian military regimes ruled with a deft touch, and rarely resorted to ruthless force. Apart from being unelected, they behaved little differently from the civilians they replaced.
The group of officers that brought Gowon to power in August 1966 formed the foundation of all succeeding military regimes until 1998. Although leadership of the regimes changed, the personalities behind the coups and regimes did not.

The 1966 cadre created successive dynastic military regimes for the next 32 years. The young non-commissioned officers (NCOs) and lieutenants, who blasted Major General Aguiyi-Ironsi from power in 1966, were the same colonels who ousted his successor, General Gowon in 1975, and they became the Brigadiers and Major-generals who overthrew President Shagari in 1983. These officers included Ibrahim Babangida, Sani Abacha, Muhammadu Buhari, Shehu Musa Yar'Adua, Aliyu Mohammed, Joshua Dogonyaro, Jerry Useni and Ibrahim Bako."

As briefly as possible, I have taken a shot at highlighting feasible and workable solutions to the certain challenges facing the nation. Solutions! They are inexhaustible. Many social commentators, policy analysts, sociologists, concerned citizens and various stakeholders have in times past proffered some ingenious solution or another. One critical thing however that is missing, and is the fulcrum upon which everything rests is political will. Be warned that I don't pretend to have any answers out of the blues. Aside from examining the basis for our disjointedness as a nation (via historical antecedents), I have simply put together ideas propounded by keen research analysts and added my own views.

In chapters 1, 2 and 3, we walk through the country's historical antecedents, taking the reader through a brief journey of colonialism, coups and societal degradation.

In chapter 4, we talk about the challenges of nationhood on the Journey to Infrastructure viz-a-viz power, transportation and industry.

Chapter 5 takes a cursory look at the Nigerian economy as well as the cankerworm of corruption that is threatening to bring her down.

In chapter 6, the economic miracle called Singapore as an archetype that can be roleplayed to produce the Nigerian miracle is examined.

Finally, the first line in the introduction to Greg Mills' book *Why Africa is Poor,* states categorically that Africa is poor because her leaders have chosen the path of poverty. Hence, in the last chapter, we engage critical reasoning and explore down-to-earth ideas that once enforced can put the country back on track.

Above all, the intent here is to inspire citizens to seek what they can do for themselves. I must confess that this might prove an uphill and hard task because it seems as though Nigerians are not ready to create the critical mass for birthing restoration (I cringe at using the word *change*). Nonetheless, hard does not translate to impossibility – nation-building has never in the history of mankind been the stuff of weaklings and the fainthearted. I am definite that with enough political will and discipline, the restoration is possible.

This is my token contribution to the discourse on propelling this Nigeria, this slumbering giant, onwards to the path of prominence and pride.

Happy reading!
Rufai Oseni

Chapter 1

The Genesis

When the colonialists landed ship on a bustling and joyous African continent, they sought possibilities of trade and market considerations. The Portuguese started the incursion and made trading arrangements across the various coastal areas of Africa. Prior to this time, in the 1400s, Africa had developed thriving empires, from the Ghanaian empire to the Malian empire under Mansa Musa, which culminated to the development and prosperity of Timbuktu.

Timbuktu (1100-1300)
Timbuktu was founded around 1100 AD by Sanhaja desert nomads. It was also the era of the

dominance of the Ghanaian Empire. Customarily, the Sanhaja nomads camped near Niger River in the dry season and took their animals inlands to graze during the rainy season. Typically, whenever the nomads were away on grazing sojourns, their belongings were entrusted to their slaves. Prominent amongst these was one called Buktu. The campsite later became known as Tim Buktu meaning 'Well of Buktu'.

What began as a semi-permanent nomadic community, with time, evolved into a town and ultimately became a city of permanent settlement. In the nascent Timbuktu, the rule of law held sway as it had a very vibrant societal structure undergirded with intense passion for intellectual development.

Having become grounded as a citadel of trade as well as learning, there was continuous intermingling of ideas and thoughts, which eventually led to the formation of the Sankore University in 1400AD. This university became a hub for scholars and intellectuals; notable amongst them was Ahmed Baba, who contributed a lot to the development of Timbuktu.

Aside scholastic activities, leadership also had a great role to play in the evolution of Timbuktu. Under the Askiya Dynasty, Timbuktu benefited immensely. This is what the Tarikh al Fettash said: "One cannot count either the virtues or the qualities of [Askiya Muhammad I]. Such is his excellent politics, his kindness towards his subjects and his solicitude towards the poor. One cannot find his equal either among those who preceded him, nor those who followed. He had a great affection for the scholars, saints and men of learning."

Askiya was a devout Muslim, so with Islam dominating the cities, and traditional religions dominating the villages, the rural dwellers and villagers did not necessarily benefit from the Askiya Dynasty. The glorious Timbuktu Empire finally ended when a partnership of the Moroccans and the British Empire conquered it in 1591.

While all of this was happening, present day Nigeria was already in shape in the form of powerful kingdoms, empires and self-existing regions.

NIGERIA 770 A.D. – 16TH CENTURY

In the history of what is now present day Nigeria, in the southern region, the earliest Ijaw settlements were discovered as far back as 770AD. It was the same time that the Nok civilization and culture, was having full preeminence.

By 800 AD, there was already a mega-state at Igbo-Ukwu, which had a complex social structure, and produced copious artifacts including bronzes. This was the Nri Kingdom, located southeast of present day Nigeria.

Concurrently in that era, Yoruba civilization was already well-established, based on thirteen farming villages centered at Ilé-Ifẹ̀, western region of the nation. By 1200, Ilé-Ifẹ̀ is widely reported to have become a Yoruba metropolis.

The NRI Kingdom

The Nri kingdom is considered a center of Igbo civilization and culture. Nri and Aguleri, where the Umueri-Igbo creation myth originates, are in the territory of the Umu-Eri clan, who trace their lineages back to the patriarchal king-figure, Eri. Eri's origin is unclear, though he has been described either as an Igala warrior or a "sky being sent by Chukwu (God). He is credited with first giving societal order to the people of Anambra. Nri history may be divided into six main periods: the pre-Eri period (before 948 CE), the Eri period (948–1041 CE), migration and unification (1042–1252 CE), the heyday of Nri hegemony (1253–1679 CE), hegemony decline and collapse (1677–1936 CE) and the Socio-culture Revival (1974–Present).

Archaeological evidence suggests that Nri hegemony in Igboland may go back as far as the 9th century and royal burials have been unearthed, dating to at least the 10th century. Eri, the god-like founder of Nri, is believed to have settled the region around 948, with other related Igbo cultures following after in the 13th century. The first eze Nri (King of Nri), Ìfikuánim, follows directly after him. According to Igbo oral tradition, his reign started in 1043. At least one historian puts Ìfikuánim's reign much later, around 1225 CE.

In 1911, the names of 19 eze Nri were recorded, but the list is not easily converted into chronological terms because of long interregnums between installations. Tradition held that at least seven years would pass upon the death of the eze Nri before a successor could be determined. The interregnum served as a period of divination of signs from a deceased eze Nri, who is said to communicate his choice of successor from the great beyond in the seven or more years ensuing upon his death. Regardless of the actual date, this period marks the beginning of Nri kingship as a centralized institution.

Colonization and expansion of the kingdom of Nri was achieved by sending mbùríchi, or converts, to other settlements. Allegiance to the eze Nri was obtained not by military force but through ritual oaths. Religious authority was vested in the local king, and ties were maintained by the traveling mbùríchi. By the 14th century, Nri influence extended well beyond the nuclear northern Igbo region to Igbo settlements on the west bank of the Niger and communities affected by the Benin Empire. There is strong evidence to indicate Nri influence went well beyond the Igbo region to Benin and Southern Igala areas like Idah. At its height, the kingdom of Nri had influence over roughly a third of Igboland and beyond. It reached its furthest extent between 1100 and 1400.

Nri's hegemony over much of Igboland lasted from the reigns of the fourth eze Nri to that of the ninth. After that, patterns of conflict emerged that existed from the tenth to the fourteenth reigns, which probably reflected the monetary importance of the slave trade. Outside-world influence was not going to be halted by native religious doctrine in the face of the slave trade's economic opportunities. Nri hegemony declined after the 18th century. Still, it survived in a much-reduced and weakened form until 1911, when British troops forced the reigning eze Nri to renounce the ritual power of the religion known as the ìkénga, ending the kingdom of Nri as a political power.

The Yoruba and Benin Empires

The same era saw the Yoruba Empire that spanned towards Dahomey well in form and shape. The story is told of Lamurudi, who came from Saudi Arabia, and bore Oduduwa, the progenitor of the Yoruba race, and Oduduwa in turn begat Okanbi. It was Okanbi, who sent 7 of his sons to be kings in different areas spanning the kingdom. It should be noted that Okanbi had eight children; seven borne to him by his "legal" wife, namely Onipopo of Popo, Onisabe of Sabe, Alara of Ilara, Ajero of Ijero, Orangun of Oke-Ila, Owa Obokun Ajibogun of Ijesaland and Oranmiyan; and one (Ooni of Ife) by his slave-turned-wife, Orunto. By 1200, Ile-Ife was already a full-blown metropolis with buoyant economy in architecture, farming, and bronze works. A testament to this is the *Opa Oranimyan*, which has been there since the Ife pre-classical period.

As for the Benin Empire, there are many contentions about its origin. Notably, is one that says Oranmiyan started the empire which later snowballed into Igodomigodo, its first historical name, as called by its inhabitants - present-day Edo people.
According to Edo oral history, the name Igodomigodo was given to the kingdom by Igodo, the first Ogiso (King). The original people and founders of the Benin Empire, the Edo people, were initially ruled by the Ogiso (Kings of the Sky). The Ogiso era, started by Igodo, was the first dynasty of what would later be known as the Benin Empire (which itself existed from around 1180 until 1897).

The rulers or kings were commonly known as *Bish*. The first Ogiso wielded much influence and gained popularity as a good ruler. He died after a long reign and was succeeded by Ere, his eldest son. In the 12th century, a great palace intrigue and battle for power erupted between the crown prince, Ekaladerhan, son of Ogiso Owodo and his young paternal uncle. In anger over an oracle, Prince Ekaladerhan left the royal court with his warriors. When his old father, the Ogiso died, the exiled Prince Ekaladerhan was sentenced to death as a result of the palace intrigues but set free on his way to execution, upon which he wandered into the forest and died at a place called Ugheton.
That ended the Ogiso dynasty as the people and royal kingmakers preferred the prince as natural next-in-line to rule.

After the death of Ogiso Owodo, the Igodomigodo elders sought for a ruler in Ile-Ife, which at the time, was an organised and established Yoruba kingdom. Oduduwa grudgingly granted them Oranmiyan, his grandson but Oranmiyan was resisted by the Ogiso chiefs. Hence, he took up abode in the palace built for him at Usama by the elders (now a coronation shrine). Soon after his arrival, he married a beautiful lady, Erinmwinde, daughter of Osa-nego, who was the ninth Enogie (Duke) of Ego. The couple had a son. After some years of residence there, he renounced his office, remarking that the community was *Ile Ibinu* -Yoruba words meaning a land of vexation (by which name the place was afterward known).
He held that only a child born, trained and educated in the arts and mysteries of the land could reign over the people.

Consequently, Oranmiyan caused his son, born to him by Erinmwinde, to be made king in his stead, while he returned to Ile-Ife. The problem however, was that his son, whom he left behind, was deaf and dumb. Hence, the elders did recourse to Oranmiyan, who then gave them charmed seeds (*omo ayo*) which he purported would heal the young lad, and frequently, the little monarch played with the seeds alongside his peers at Ego, his mother's hometown. One day, whilst playing with the seeds, his tongue strings loosed and he burst out unexpectedly in Yoruba, "Owo mika" (meaning my hands have caught it). This is why everyone to be coronated as Oba of Benin must stay seven days in Usama and announce his name at the town of Ego.

Oranmiyan was also the founder of Oyo Empire, where he ruled supreme as the first Alaafin of Oyo, then Oba of Benin and proceeded to Ile-Ife to become the 6th Ooni of Ife while his descendants ruled in Ile-Ife, Oyo and Benin.

By the 15th century, Benin had expanded into a thriving city-state. The twelfth Oba in line, Oba Ewuare the Great (1440–1473) would expand the city-state to an empire.
It was during his reign that the kingdom's administrative centre, Ubinu, began to be known as Benin City by the Portuguese, and later to be adopted by the locals. Before then, due to the pronounced ethnic diversity at the kingdom's headquarters, the earlier name ('Ubinu') by a tribe of the Edos was colloquially spoken as "Bini" by the mix of Itsekhiri, Esan, Ika, Ijaw Edo, and Urhobo living together in the royal administrative centre of the kingdom. The Portuguese would write this down as Benin City. Though, farther Edo clans such as the Itsekiris and the Urhobos still referred to the city as Ubini up till the late 19th century.

Even though the Ogiso era would be replaced by the Oba's, the system of rule of the Oba even through the golden age of the kingdom, was still loosely based after the Ogiso dynasty, which was military and royal protection in exchange of use of resources and implementation of taxes paid to the royal administrative centre. The name of the kingdom was changed from Igodomigodo to Edo by Oba Eweka I.
Language and culture was not enforced but remained heterogeneous and localized according to each group within the kingdom, though a local "Enogie" (duke) was often appointed by the Oba for specified ethnic areas.
The Benin Empire spanned about 90,000km at its peak and had a vibrant economy of bronze work, with a unified and effective system of government and documented history in its arts. All this was cut short when Oba Ovonrawen was exiled to Calabar in 1897 and the Benin Empire was judiciously looted by the British. Herein is the list of the Obas of Benin.

- **Pre-Imperial Obas (pre-1180 - 1440)**
  *The dates of reigns of these early kings are highly uncertain.
  Oranmiyan
  Eweka I (1180–1246)
  Uwuakhuahen (1246–1250)
  Henmihen (1250–1260)
  Ewedo (1260–1274)
  Oguola (1274–1287)
  Edoni (1287–1292)
  Udagbedo (1292–1329)

Ohen (1329–1366)
Egbeka (1366–1397)
Orobiru (1397–1434)
Uwaifiokun (1434–1440)

- **Obas of the Benin Empire (1440–1897)**

*There is some uncertainty in the dates of the reigns of some of the earlier warrior kings.

Ewuare I (1440–1473)
Ezoti (1473–1474)
Olua (1475–1480)
Ozolua (1480–1504)
Esigie (1504–1547)
Orhogbua (1547–1580)
Ehengbuda (1580–1602)
Ohuan (1602–1656)
Ohenzae (1656–1661)
Akenzae (1661–1669)
Akengboi (1669–1675)
Akenkpaye (1675–1684)
Akengbedo (1684–1689)
Ore-Oghene (1689–1701)
Ewuakpe (1701–1712)
Ozuere (1712–1713)
Akenzua I (1713–1740)
Eresoyen (1740–1750)
Akengbuda (1750–1804)
Obanosa (1804–1816)
Ogbebo (1816)
Osemwende (1816–1848)
Adolo (1848–1888)
Ovonramwen Nogbaisi (1888–1914) (exiled to Calabar by the British in 1897)

- **Post-Imperial Obas of Benin (1914–Present)**

Eweka II (1914–1933)
Akenzua II (1933–1978)
Erediauwa (1979–2016)
Ewuare II (2016–)
Source: Wikipedia (List of Obas of the Benin Empire)

As the Nri kingdom, Benin Empire and Yoruba Empire thrived, the Islamic empire of Bornu in the was blooming *pari passu.*

The Islamic State of Bornu (1100)

The growth of the Islamic state of Bornu was a historical contact point in Nigeria's history as it was the fundamental cohesion of the northern region. The British did find it easy to meander the task of governance because of the hitherto prevalent structure in the north and all of this stemmed from the Islamic state of Bornu.

From the 1380s to 1893, the Bornu Empire was the entirety of what is now the northeastern Nigeria. It was a continuation of the great Kanem Empire founded centuries earlier by the Sayfawa Dynasty. In time it would become even larger than Kanem, incorporating areas that are today parts of Chad, Niger, Sudan, and Cameroon.

Even in Bornu, the Sayfawa Dynasty's troubles persisted. During the first three-quarters of the 15th century, for example, fifteen mais occupied the throne. Then, around 1455, Mai Ali Dunamami defeated his rivals and began the consolidation of Bornu. He built a fortified capital at Ngazargamu (in present-day Nigeria), to the west of Lake Chad. This was the first permanent home a Sayfawa mai had enjoyed in a century. So successful was the Sayfawa rejuvenation that by the early 16th century, Mai Ali Gaji (1455–1487) was able to defeat the Bulala and retake Njimi, the former capital. The empire's leaders, however, remained at Ngazargamu because its lands were more productive agriculturally and better suited to the raising of cattle. Ali Gaji was the first ruler of the empire to assume the title of Caliph.

With control over both capitals, the Sayfawa dynasty became more powerful than ever. The two states were merged, but political authority still rested in Bornu. Kanem-Bornu peaked during the reign of the statesman Mai Idris Alooma (c. 1571–1603).

Idris Alooma is remembered for his military skills, administrative reforms, and Islamic piety. His innovations included the employment of fixed military camps (with walls); permanent sieges and "scorched earth" tactics, where soldiers burned everything in their path; armored horses and riders; and the use of Berber camelry, Kotoko boatmen, and iron-helmeted musketeers, trained by Turkish military advisers. His active diplomacy featured relations with Tripoli, Egypt, and the Ottoman Empire, which sent a 200-member ambassadorial party across the desert to Alooma's court at Ngazargamu. Alooma also signed what was probably the first written treaty or cease-fire in Chadian history.

Alooma introduced a number of legal and administrative reforms based on his religious beliefs and Islamic law (sharia). He sponsored the construction of numerous mosques and made a pilgrimage (hajj) to Mecca, where he arranged for the establishment of a hostel to be used by pilgrims from his empire. As with other dynamic politicians, Alooma's reformist goals led him to seek loyal and competent advisers and allies, and he frequently relied on slaves who had been educated in noble homes. Alooma regularly sought advice from a council composed of heads of the most important clans... and reinforced political alliances through appropriate marriages. (Alooma himself was the son of a Kanuri father and a Bulala mother).

Kanem-Bornu under Alooma was strong and wealthy. Government revenue came from tribute (or booty, if the recalcitrant people had to be conquered), sales of slaves, and duties on and participation in trans-Saharan trade. Unlike West Africa, the Chadian region did not have gold. Still, it was central to one of the most convenient trans-Saharan routes. Between Lake Chad and Fezzan lay a sequence of well-spaced wells and oases, and from Fezzan there were easy connections to North Africa and the Mediterranean Sea. Many products were sent north, including natron (sodium carbonate), cotton, kola nuts, ivory, ostrich feathers, perfume, wax, and hides, but the most important of all were slaves. Imports included salt, horses, silks, glass, muskets, and copper.

Alooma took keen interest in trade and other economic matters. He is credited with having the roads cleared, designing better boats for Lake Chad, introducing standard units of measure for grain, and moving farmers into new lands. In addition, he improved the ease and security of transit through the empire with the goal of making it so safe that "a lone woman clad in gold might walk with none to fear but God."

European Invasion in the Territories

The year 1450 marked the beginning of European contact on the Atlantic coast. By 1500, the nominally Muslim Hausa kingdoms were already established in what is now known as northern Nigeria. Same goes for all the empires and kingdoms – Benin, Yoruba, Nri – that make up present day Nigeria. And as highlighted in the foregoing, they were all already established civilizations in their own rights.

Chapter 2

Vanguard of Revolutions

Trade and commerce boomed across the Trans-Saharan routes between Europeans and the West African natives. However, there were issues of subjugation and manipulation from the economic visitors. The indigenous people would not take it lying low. In a short time, it would seem that the people inhabiting the Nigerian territories would constantly be in the vanguard of fighting for their rights. And so it was. Here, two epitome stories come to mind.

The first, being the brazen attempt at escape from slavery by a group of slaves of majorly Igbo extraction. History has it that in May 1803, a shipload of captive West Africans, upon surviving the middle passage, were landed by U.S.-paid captors in Savannah by slave ship, to be auctioned off at one of the local slave markets. The ship's enslaved passengers included a number of Igbo people from what is now Nigeria. The Igbo were known by planters and slaves of the American South for being fiercely independent and resistant to chattel slavery. The Igbo slaves (75 in no.) were bought to be used as forced labor on plantations in St. Simons Island at the cost of $100 each, by agents of John Couper and Thomas Spalding.

The chained slaves were packed under the deck of a small vessel named *The Schooner York* to be shipped to the island (other sources say the voyage took place aboard The Morovia, During this voyage the Igbo slaves rose up in rebellion, taking control of the ship and drowning their captors in the process causing the grounding of the Morovia in Dunbar Creek at the site now locally known as Igbo Landing.

The following sequence of events is unclear, as there are several versions concerning the revolt's development, some of which are considered mythological. Apparently, the Africans went ashore and subsequently, under the direction of a high Igbo chief among them, walked in unison into the creek singing in the Igbo language "The water spirit brought us, the water spirit will take us home". They thereby accepted the protection of their god, *chukwu* and death over the alternative of slavery. Roswell King, a white overseer on the nearby Pierce Butler plantation, wrote one of the only contemporary accounts of the incident which states that as soon as the Igbo landed on St. Simons Island, they took to the swamp, committing suicide by walking into Dunbar Creek.

A 19th-century account of the event identifies the captain by the surname Patterson and names Roswell King as the person, who recovered the bodies of the drowned. A letter describing the event written by Savannah slave dealer, William Mein states that the Igbo walked into the marsh, where 10 to 12 drowned, while some were "salvaged" by bounty hunters who received $10 a head from Spalding and Couper. According to some sources, survivors of the Igbo rebellion were taken to Cannon's Point on St. Simons Island and Sapelo Island.

The Aba Women War

A second important anecdote which validates the resilient Nigerian spirit is the famous Aba women war, which the British deliberately skewed as a riot, undoubtedly to mitigate its severity and dampen its intensity, for reasons best known to them.

It goes that prior to the 1st of January 1900, the various empires that make up present-day Nigeria (as highlighted in the previous chapter) had been trading hubs. The Royal Niger company (RNC) under the management of Sir George Tubman Goldie and the Germans held sway but all of this came crumbling like a pack of cards, when incursions were made by other colonial nations that equally understood the economic viability of the regions that now make up modern day Nigeria.

Trade disputes became rampant. This was a pain in the heart of the British, due to perpetual fights and skirmishes. Tubman, who was the major trade principality alongside various partners felt threatened, as was the groundnut pyramids and palm oil trade. The juiciness of African fruits was almost causing civil strife between the European partners (which they would call a world war). However, in order to bring sanity to the situation, a certain skilled German statesman by name Bismarck, who had taken dominant status in European leadership, called the partners to a meeting to avoid the Night of long Knives. This was what led to the famed Berlin Conference.

- **The Berlin Conference**

The Berlin Conference of 1884–1885 marked the climax of the European competition for territory in Africa, a process commonly known as the Scramble for Africa. During the 1870s and early 1880s European nations such as Great Britain, France, and Germany began looking to Africa for natural resources for their growing industrial sectors as well as a potential market for the goods these factories produced. As a result, these governments sought to safeguard their commercial interests in Africa and began sending scouts to the continent to secure treaties from indigenous peoples or their supposed representatives. Similarly, Belgium's King Leopold II, who aspired to increase his personal wealth by acquiring African territory, hired agents to lay claim to vast tracts of land in central Africa. To protect Germany's commercial interests, German Chancellor Otto von Bismarck, who was otherwise uninterested in Africa, felt compelled to stake claims to African land.

Inevitably, the scramble for territory led to conflict among European powers, particularly between the British and French in West Africa; Egypt, the Portuguese, and British in East Africa; and the French and King Leopold II in central Africa. Rivalry between Great Britain and France led Bismarck to intervene, and in late 1884 he called a meeting of European powers in Berlin. In the subsequent meetings, Great Britain, France, Germany, Portugal, and King Leopold II negotiated their claims to African territory, which were then formalized and mapped. During the conference the leaders also agreed to allow free trade among the colonies and established a framework for negotiating future European claims in Africa. Neither the Berlin Conference itself nor the framework for future negotiations provided any say for the peoples of Africa over the partitioning of their homelands.

The Berlin Conference did not initiate European colonization of Africa, but it did legitimate and formalize the process. In addition, it sparked new interest in Africa. Following the close of the conference, European powers expanded their claims in Africa such that by 1900, European states had claimed nearly 90 percent of African territory.

Despite the major gains of the Berlin conference, Goldie Tubman's business never remained the same. It was a constant struggle for relevance and the business and its assets were finally handed over to the British government after the Parliament intervened. The final arrangement was done on the 1st of January 1900 and Goldie Tubman was paid off approximately £900,000. Swiftly, the British government commenced operations and rapidly gained grounds as Nigeria officially became part of British overseas territories.

By the year 1914, Lord Lugard, who was then appointed Governor, amalgamated the Southern and Northern protectorates to form the nation called Nigeria, thus being its first governor. However, subsequently owing to the fact that the people felt certain rights were being trampled on, frictions emerged at various places; a palpable one being the Aba women's war of 1929.

- **Aba Women War**

The "riots" or the war, led by women in the provinces of Calabar and Owerri in southeastern Nigeria in November and December of 1929, became known as the "Aba Women's Riots of 1929" in British colonial history, or as the "Women's War" in Igbo history. Thousands of Igbo women organized a massive revolt against the policies imposed by British colonial administrators in southeastern Nigeria, touching off the most serious challenge to British rule in the history of the colony. The "Women's War" took months for the government to suppress and became a historic example of feminist and anti-colonial protest.

The roots of the riots evolved from January 1, 1914, when the first Nigerian colonial governor, Lord Lugard, instituted the system of indirect rule in Southern Nigeria. Under this plan British administrators would rule locally through "warrant chiefs," essentially Igbo individuals appointed by the governor. Traditionally Igbo chiefs had been elected.

Within a few years the appointed warrant chiefs became increasingly oppressive. They seized property, imposed draconian local regulations, and began imprisoning anyone who openly criticized them. Although much of the anger was directed against the warrant chiefs, most Nigerians knew the source of their power, British colonial administrators. Colonial administrators added to the local sense of grievance when they announced plans to impose special taxes on the Igbo market women. These women were responsible for supplying the food to the growing urban populations in Calabar, Owerri, and other Nigerian cities. They feared the taxes would drive many of the market women out of business and seriously disrupt the supply of food and non-perishable goods available to the populace.

In November of 1929, thousands of Igbo women congregated at the Native Administration centers in Calabar and Owerri as well as smaller towns to protest both the warrant chiefs and the taxes on the market women. Using the traditional practice of censoring men through all night song and dance ridicule (often called "sitting on a man"), the women chanted and danced, and in some locations forced warrant chiefs to resign their positions. The women also attacked European owned stores and Barclays Bank and broke into prisons and released prisoners. They also attacked Native Courts run by colonial officials, burning many of them to the ground. Colonial Police and troops were called in. They fired into the crowds that had gathered at Calabar and Owerri, killing more than 50 women and wounding over 50 others. During the two month "war" at least 25,000 Igbo women were involved in protests against British officials.

The Aba Women's war prompted colonial authorities to drop their plans to impose a tax on the market women, and to curb the power of the warrant chiefs. The women's uprising is seen as the first major challenge to British authority in Nigeria and West Africa during the colonial period.

Notably, the Aba women riot was a landmark event, majorly because it would later give Nigeria's future independence fighters the impetus to push for their dues and rights. The story of the Aba women remains a stark reminder of the capability of Nigerians to push for what they believe in, when they so choose. It was a mandate of impetus - sort of like a **Magna Carta**. Prior to the Aba women riot, the Clifford constitution had ceded some rights to Nigerians.

The Trajectory to Independence

The clamour for civil liberties, constitutional rights and civil rights began to come to the forefront challenging in undertones, the instruments of the colonial government's rules and policies. Resultantly, the British colonialists sought to improve the status quo as constitution upon constitution was drafted to address clamours and injustices whilst they (colonialists) held on tightly to the reins of power.

- **The Clifford Constitution of 1922**

After Lord Lugard, the first governor of the amalgamated Nigeria was recalled by the British government, Sir Hugh Clifford was appointed in his stead. The new helmsman took the liberty to draft up a new constitution in place of the one that was in use (created by his predecessor). The Clifford Constitution of 1922 disposed the Nigerian Council of Lord Lugard (1914) and set up a new legislative council for the Southern Protectorate. The membership of the Clifford legislative council was 46. Twenty- seven out of the 46 members were officials while 19 were unofficial members. Ten out of the 19 unofficial members were Nigerians and out of the 10 unofficial Nigerians, 4 were elected, 3 from Lagos and 1 from Calabar. The remaining six were appointed by the governor. The Northern protectorate was excluded from the council. The governor continued to govern the North by proclamation.

The Clifford constitution of 1922 established the elective principle for the first time in Nigeria. However, the elective principle was limited to male adults who had resided in Nigeria for over 12 months, with gross annual income of 100 pounds.
The Clifford constitution also gave way to the establishment of political parties in Nigeria. Thus, in 1923, Herbert Macaulay became the first Nigerian to found a political party, the Nigerian National Democratic Party (NNDP). Principally, the Clifford Constitution gave room for more indigenous participation and representation in the government than the 1914 constitution.

- **Main Features of the Clifford Constitution of 1922**
  * Elective principle to elect desired person into the Legislative council. NB:- Only an individual earning £100 annually can vote and be voted for. NCBWA struggled for the granting of the elective principle in Nigeria.

  * All colonial governors were to report to the Secretary of State for colonies, who was a cabinet minister in Britain.

  * The Executive council was an all-European council. No Nigerian was included i.e. Nigerians were not part of the decision-making body.

  * The Legislative council consists of 46 members of which 27 were official and 19 were unofficial.

  * The North was ruled by proclamation coming from the governor.

  * Formation of political parties e.g. NNDP of Herbert Macaulay.

  * Establishment of Newspapers e.g. The West African Pilot and Lagos Daily News

In the year 1937, Nnamdi Azikiwe set up the first Nigerian newspaper, *The West African Pilot*. Its superior objective was to push and fight for national independence. Later on, other dailies would spring up to join in the agitation for self-actualization. This pressure build-up led to actions by the British government skewed towards ensuring the self-governance the Nigerians craved for became a reallty.

Finally, in 1954, all the struggles paid off with the drafting and activation of the Lyttleton Constitution.

- **The Lyttleton Constitution of 1954**
In 1954, the Lyttleton Constitution declared Nigeria a federation consisting of three regions, the

federal territories of Lagos and the Southern Cameroons. A goal of the constitution was to promote regional autonomy.
It was named after Oliver Lyttleton, the then secretary of the colonies in London.
The Lyttleton Constitution was as a result of perceived defections in the Macpherson Constitution of 1951. To correct these defections, in 1953, a constitutional conference had been called in London, with about 20 delegates, mainly representatives of the political parties that won the elections conducted in the country. Another constitutional conference was later held in Lagos.

Significantly, the 1954 constitution can be said to be a text designed to relieve any tension derived from the polarizing effect of a quasi-federal political structure, giving regions more powers. It maintained the 50/50 distribution between the North and the South in the federal legislature. Also, members were to be elected directly from various constituencies in Nigeria.

The constitution delegates a few services, 68 in total, to the central government and the House of Representatives under the federal legislative list. These powers included aviation, banking, census, copyright, currency, customs, defense, external relations, immigration, mining, police, railway, etc. On the concurrent list, the constitution made provision for dual roles between the federal and regional government, and the residual list was awarded to the regional governments. The constitution made provision for the selection of regional ministers from the regional House of Assemblies and the premier being the leader of dominant party in the legislature. The government and individual ministers in the regions maintained power by obtaining the confidence of the majority of members in the regional assembly.

Of paramount note is the fact that the Lyttleton Constitution created strong impetus for the independence movement that led to the Lancaster House Conferences. The Lancaster House Conferences in London 1957 and 1958 were the meetings, where the federal constitution for an independent Nigeria was prepared. These meetings were presided over by the British Colonial Secretary, and Nigerian delegates were selected to represent each region to reflect various shades of opinion. The delegation was led by Abubakar Tafawa Balewa of the Northern People's Congress (NPC), and included party leaders - Obafemi Awolowo of the Action Group, Nnamdi Azikiwe of the NCNC, Eyo Ita of the NIP (National Independence Party) and Ahmadu Bello of the NPC – as well as the premiers of the Western, Eastern, and Northern regions; Chiefs of the Northern Region - Sir Muhammadu Sanusi, Emir of Kano and Alhaji Usman Nagogo, Emir of Katsina; Chiefs of the Western Region - Sir Adesoji Aderemi and Oba Aladesanmi; and Chiefs of the Eastern Region - Chief Nyong Essien of Uyo and Chief S. E. Onukogu.

Independence: Too early?

When independence finally came in 1960, there was a lot of joy and hope that Nigeria was going to be a leader and a beacon of hope, but there were strong, pungent militating factors like ethnicity, which had been perpetuated by the British. When the Southern and Northern protectorates were brought together in 1914, the British were unwilling to get into the murky water of building a nation so they encouraged a divide-and-rule mindset. The British colonialists encouraged individualism amongst the regions, as long as they met tax returns, made gains and the financial remittal quota was met. The British saw no need to integrate the regions.

This was further heightened with the formation of political parties - Northern Peoples' Congress (NPC) which was strictly for the North; a westerner would never be the head of such a party. Action Group (AG) was a western Party, NCNC (National Council of Nigerian Citizens) was strictly for the East. This belied their names which reflected a nationalistic outlook.
As a result, in the true sense of the word, there were no Nigerians and the people (regions) themselves were not thinking or contemplating building up 'a Nigerian people'. This caused not a little problem. It became and still is, a pivotal challenge which for decades threatens the unity of the contraption called Nigeria. Sir Tafawa Balewa voiced this, as Awolowo also did in his book, *Path to Nigerian Freedom*, "What our early leaders should have done was to follow the instructions of Massimo d'azeglio, who stated, 'We have built Italy. Now it's time to build Italians.'"

Provincialism was palpable as the early leaders were only concerned about their regions. NPC leader, Adamu Bello was quoted to have said, "I would rather be Sultan of Sokoto than president of Nigeria." This was even in the 1950s, as individuals like Adamu Bello were against early independence. On occasion, this led to Northern leaders being jeered in Lagos. This humiliation never left the northern memory.
Mistrust was rife amongst the early leaders. A game of musical chairs started, heightened by riots and mass electoral problems. Young military idealists were watching.
The situation was tense as rancour and in-fighting among political parties in various regions, such as the famous fight between Akintola and Awolowo had started for supremacy, and led to numerous riots. The military saw this rancour amongst politicians and it had always been somehow obvious that the military was going to be part of politics in Nigeria but nobody knew that the likes of David Ejoor, who led the change of guards at independence, would play an important role in the military incursion.

Another battle for supremacy occurred in 1959 at the Federal elections, where Chief Awolowo's Action Group (AG) had made a lot of gains and astounded other regions. The 1959 elections was the beginning of election dispute and malpractices in Nigeria. The ensuing violence was of biblical proportions, destroying anything that stood in its path.
As stated in Awolowo's book *Adventures in Power*, Awolowo's AG's gains had soured the Sardauna and in a *Sunday Express* report of 20th December, 1959, it was stated as quoted by the Sardauna, "I shall divide Nigeria into two and hand them to my lieutenants."
The free-for-all then started as various AG members were hurt in the north and some were left for dead. The story is told of Chief Rosiji, the Action Group's secretary, who was ambushed in Raba.

Unrelenting also in the east, the strife saw Dr. K.O Mbadiwe fall out with Dr. Nnamdi Azikiwe, leader of the NCNC. Mbadiwe went on to form another party known as the Democratic Party of Nigerian Citizens. This party later sought alliance with the Action Group, a step which led to another civil strife in the east. In the end, the federal formation of government was an NPC-

NCNC one. Tafawa Balewa and Nnamdi Azikiwe were handed power. The Sardauna had declined being president and the position was handed over to his deputy. The Action Group was in opposition.

This set the stage for modern Nigeria. It also led to further scrambling, as the leading coalition wanted more autonomy particularly since the western region was juicy. All this wrangling was setting the stage for a climax which led to not just the first coup but a season of coups and countercoups.

Chapter 3

Of Coups and Riots

According to Max Siollun, "The army's journey into politics was akin to sitting an exam prior to attending lectures. The 1980s Nigerian army was a legacy of the civil war during which mass military recruitment swelled the military's manpower from 10,000 in 1966 to approximately 250,000 by the end of the war in 1970. A swollen military became a drain on government finances, and an internal security risk. Nigeria faced no external military threat from a foreign power, thus the army's role was largely devoted to the suppression of communal riots and international peacekeeping missions. With no external enemies to fight, military heroism tended to be sought in the political arena rather than on the battlefield."

A Season of Coups

Sufficiently, the atmosphere in the political terrain created ample impetus for young idealists in the Army, who thought they had solutions. Since the politicians did not seem to be ready to behave themselves and lead as they ought, the military was ready to put things in perspective for them. Kaduna Nzeogwu led the way.

In his book, *On Why We Struck*, Adewale Ademoyega (one of the five military officers, who led the 1966 coup) penned:

> *The political imbroglio had been a veritable footing for the military. The dirty politicking of the NPC, NNDP, MDF, UPGA, NCNC, NNA and other alliances led to real disruptions and riots in the western region. Very popular amongst them in Oct 1964 was the "wetie" riots - houses of chief political actors were "wetted" with petrol and set ablaze. The census and regional elections also spurred young revolutionaries in the army like Ifeanjuna and Nzeogwu to take over.*
> *These young men had faced the segregation and northernization of the army that saw 50% of the intakes of the army of northern extraction.*

All of this led the way for the first coup in 1966. During this coup, the critical mass of the political elite was killed. Tribal sentiments ensued; an Igbo man was in charge. Ironsi was said to be partial by not punishing the coup plotters, who were of the Igbo extraction. This led to a cleansing in the army. Soldiers of northern extraction started killing their southern counterparts. A counter coup ensued the same year, with Aguiyi Ironsi and other top military officers being killed.

Spiraling, these led to unimaginable, malicious riots in the north. The intensity of the crisis became unbearable and Ojukwu had to meet with Gowon in Aburi, Ghana for settlement but it was to no avail. Consequently, the civil war started in 1967 and Nigeria never remained the same. This unfortunate event, broke, not only every vestige of nationhood remaining, it would also open the door for various riots, uprisings and unrests, and quite significantly, deepen mistrust among Nigerian citizens across all ethnicities for a long time to come.

The Army's first foray into the polity might have been honorably motivated, albeit objectionable. However, at the Army's second incursion into the Nigerian political terrain, the air was different as Siollun notes, "The nature of military governance changed greatly during the 1980s. Coups became motivated by a desire for personal gain, rather than by altruism or ideology."
There was no need for a soothsayer or a crystal ball. The military was now hell-bent on wielding political power. This being the case, numerous military officers took to obtuse self-aggrandizement and sleaze from government treasury, thus becoming stupendously rich from the coups, leaving the country's fortunes tethered on the brink of jeopardy and collapse.
The military held power in Nigeria until 1996, under Ibrahim Babangida, who handed over to an interim government, headed by Chief Ernest Sonekan.

RELIGIOUS RIOTS IN NIGERIA

The aftermath of the First World War saw Germany lose its colonies, one of which was Cameroon, to the French, Belgian and British mandates. Cameroon was divided into French and British parts, the latter of which was further subdivided into southern and northern parts. Following a plebiscite in 1961, the Southern Cameroons elected to rejoin French Cameroon, while the Northern Cameroons opted to join Nigeria, a move which added to Nigeria's already large northern Muslim population. The territory comprises much of what is now Northeastern Nigeria, and a large part of the areas affected by past and present insurgencies.

Following the return of democratic government to Nigeria in 1999, Sharia was instituted as a main body of civil and criminal law in 9 Muslim-majority and in some parts of 3 Muslim-plurality states. This occurred when former Zamfara State governor, Ahmad Rufai Sani began the push for the institution of Sharia at state level.
The Sharia law encompasses punishments against blasphemy and apostasy. Consequently, several incidents have arisen, whereby people have been killed in response to perceived insults to Islam. Somehow, those killings were not anything out of the ordinary. Religious conflicts in Nigeria go as far back as 1953, and in the case of the town of Tafawa Balewa, to 1948.The Igbo massacre of 1966 in the north that followed the counter-coup of the same year had as a dual cause - the Igbo officers' coup and pre-existing (sectarian) tensions between the Igbos and local Muslims. This was a major factor in the Biafran secession and the resulting civil war. (Wikipedia

on Insurgency, Boko Haram)

Also, in the late 1970s and early 1980s, there was a major Islamic uprising led by Mohammed Marwa (aka Maitatsine) and his followers, Yan Tatsine, that led to several thousand deaths. After Maitatsine's death in 1980, the movement continued some five years more.
In the same decade, the erstwhile military ruler of Nigeria, General Ibrahim Babangida enrolled Nigeria in the Organisation of the Islamic Conference (OIC). This was a move which aggravated religious tensions in the country, particularly among the Christian community. In response, some in the Muslim community pointed out that certain other African member states, with smaller proportions of Muslims, have diplomatic relations with the Holy See.

In the 1980s, serious outbreaks between Christians and Muslims occurred in Kafanchan, southern Kaduna, in a border area. This was propagated by extremist Islamic leaders, who were able to rally a group of young, educated individuals that feared the nation would not be able to protect their religious group. These leaders were able to polarize their followers through speeches and public demonstrations. The activities of some of these sects has in recent times led to the loss of lives and properties as they move about destroying government facilities (particularly schools) as well as churches, which they see as legacies or replica of western cultures in their various communities. These religious campaigns have seen an increase in gun battles between members of these sects and security forces, with loss of lives witnessed on both sides. Although initially, direct conflicts between Christians and Muslims were rare, tensions did flare between the two groups as each group radicalised.

There were clashes in October 1982, when Muslim zealots in Kano were able to enforce their power in order to keep the Anglican House Church from expanding its size and power base. They saw it as a threat to the nearby mosque, even though the Anglican House Church had been there forty years prior to the building of the mosque. Additionally, two student groups in Nigeria came into contestation, namely, the Fellowship of Christian Students (FCS) and the Muslim Student Society (MSS). In one instance, an evangelical campaign organised by the FCS brought into question why one sect should dominate the campus of the Kafanchan College of Education. This squabble accelerated to the point where the Muslim students organised protests around the city and culminated in the burning of a church building at the college. The Christian majority at the college retaliated with a mob showdown, where twelve people died, several mosques were burnt and a climate of fear was created. The retaliation was pre-planned.

The role of the media cannot be glossed over in this situation as it was sufficiently exploited to propagate the ideas of the conflict, thereby radicalizing each force the more. Media was biased on each side so while outfits like the Federal Radio Corporation discussed the idea of defending Islam during this brief moment of terror, it did not report the deaths and damage caused by Muslims, galvanizing the Muslim population. Similarly, the Christian papers did not report the damage and deaths caused by Christians but rather focused on the Islamic terror. Other individuals leading these religious movements used the media to spread messages which gradually became more intolerant of other religions, and because of these religious divisions, radical Islam continues to be a factor.

Also, in 1991, the German evangelist, Reinhard Bonnke, attempted to hold a crusade in Kano. This triggered a religious riot which led to the death of about a dozen people.

The 2000s-2010s

Since the restoration of democracy in 1999, Christians have held office at the federal level, while the Muslim-dominated Northern Nigerian states have implemented strict Sharia law. Religious conflict between Muslims and Christians has erupted several times since 2000 for various reasons, often causing riots with several thousands of victims on both sides. Since 2009, the Islamist movement, Boko Haram has fought an armed rebellion against the Nigerian military, sacking villages and towns and taking thousands of lives in battles and massacres against Christians, students and others deemed to be enemies of Islam.

At Abuja in year 2000 as well as Jos, in 2001, there were riots between Christians and Muslims over the appointment of a Muslim politician, Alhaji Muktar Mohammed, as local coordinator of the federal programme for poverty eradication. Another such riot killed over 100 people in October 2001, in Kano State.

In 2002, the Nigerian journalist, Isioma Daniel wrote an article which led to demonstrations and violence that caused the deaths of over 200 in Kaduna, as well as a fatwa being placed on her life. The 2002 Miss World contest was moved from Abuja to London as a result. The rest of the first decade of the 2000s would see inter-religious violence continue in Jos and Kaduna.

In 2005, when Danish newspaper, *Jyllands-Posten* published series of cartoons of the prophet Mohammed, it was not quite ready for the worldwide backlash that would follow its publication, rippling all the way to Nigeria. The reaction to the Mohammed cartoons brought about a series of violent protests in Nigeria. Clashes between rioters and police claimed several lives, with estimates ranging from 16 to more than 100. This led to reprisal attacks in the south of the country, particularly in Onitsha, whereupon another more than a hundred lost their lives. These and countless others are the occurrences of religious riots and pandemonium in the country

The Current War of Religion

Religion has always been the opium of the masses in Nigeria. Each religion claims superiority over its counterpart. Whilst the common man is slaying his neighbour on its altar, the cunning and crafty politicians and ruling elite have learnt to deftly use this sour point to heat the polity, hoodwink the people and loot the coffers blind. Even now, as we speak, there are challenges that might create unamenable divisions and possibly disintegration, if care is not taken.

The insurgency in the northeast and middle belt spearheaded in 2009 by the radicalized Islamic sect, Boko Haram - sacking and bombing entire villages, maiming, torturing, kidnapping and raping is nothing short of savagery epitomized.

The recent spate of wanton killings occasioned by Fulani herdsmen in several parts of the country is another. The conspiracy theory is that the nomads are intent on taking over farmlands nationwide and since the sitting helmsman, President Muhammed Buhari, is of the same tribe, his hands are tied, his allegiance skewed.

These are two pressing issues that we cannot afford to treat with levity - utmost sincerity and candour are needed. The former has been politicized and tied round the neck of religion. The latter is the sacred cow of ethnicity and partly religion. Yet, security of lives and property of its citizens is a cardinal responsibility of any self-respecting government. The spontaneity and frequency of these killings portray a flagrant disregard for human life. It is not so much as that from the perpetrators' side (not excusable though) but from the part of a government that is not sufficiently proactive over security concerns in its territories.

Then there are malicious Rhetorics going round, which of course, are harmful and toxic. For instance, a certain lecturer, Professor Umar Labdo Muhammad of the Faculty of Humanities, Northwest University, Kano, recently alleged that Benue State belongs to the Fulani by right of conquest.
The University don claimed that half of Benue State is part of the Bauchi Emirate as well as half of the Adamawa Emirate. In a post on his Facebook page, Muhammad stressed that by extension, Benue is "part and parcel of Sokoto Caliphate" and as such, nobody has the right to expel Fulani from the state.
Muhammad also stated that the Fulanis are the largest single nation in the African continent and they have "remained unbeatable throughout their history."
The controversial post read thus, "Benue State belongs to the Fulani people by right of conquest. This is because half of the state is part of the Bauchi Emirate and the other half is part of the Adamawa Emirate. Benue is therefore part and parcel of the Sokoto Caliphate. So no one has the right to expel the Fulani from Benue under any guise."

Are we justifying lawlessness and disorder? Needless to say, such mischievous speaking, capable of causing untold damage and further worsening a fragile polity, should be condemned in their entirety, especially from individuals of supposed high standing. That this country does not go into flames on account of these urgent matters, again I say political will needs to be exercised.

Chapter 4

Journey to Infrastructure

According to Ayodeji Olukoju, water supply and electricity were the earliest infrastructural facilities envisaged for the cities. However, neither became a practical possibility until the late 1890s and early 1900s.The infrastructure that rapidly took off was that of railway by 1899 due to proliferation of trade. The Lagos-Abeokuta and the Kaduna railway lines were functional, but in other areas of the nation, there was substantial disregard for infrastructure.

In this piece from *Infrastructure Development and Urban Facilities in Lagos, 1861-2000*, he (Olukoju) copiously narrates the historical antecedents of our infrastructure journey:

In the late 1890s, gas lanterns were placed at certain points on the Island for the illumination of the streets. Given the inadequacy of this arrangement, a Lagos newspaper canvassed for "our streets (to be) properly lighted" as the unlit streets were said to be "in a most wretched condition at night."

Such was the concern about proper street lighting that Western-educated Lagosians were prepared to pay an indirect lighting tax to fund the illumination of the city. Such concern was heightened by the spate of burglaries in the city, at least since the 1880s, though these did not abate substantially when street lighting was introduced in 1898.

Meanwhile, the issues of urban infrastructure were of common concern regardless of racial differences in the city. Both the expatriate merchants and the Western-educated Africans in Lagos (the Saro in particular) vigorously ventilated their views in the newspapers. Their clamour did not go unheeded, for the colonial administration duly proposed infrastructure policies and the most cost-effective means of implementing them. Thus, in June 1891, acting governor George Denton drew the attention of the Secretary of State for the Colonies to "the very inferior manner in which the streets in Lagos are lighted."2 He referred to the efforts made by his predecessor, Alfred Moloney, to secure lamps best suited for street lighting in tropical countries. In addition, he forwarded a report by the acting colonial surveyor in which the latter recommended that the number of lamps should be increased from 86 to 223. However, the upkeep of each lamp would also increase from £1.14.6d to £2.10.4d. He submitted that "the effectual and thorough lighting of a Town such as Lagos is a matter of the greatest importance" and that the additional cost was compensated by the greater efficiency of the social service.

October 1893, Denton intimated the Secretary of State for the Colonies with the representation made by the Lagos Chamber of Commerce, then an all-white body, on the subject of street lighting in Lagos. He conceded that street lighting in Lagos was "most defective" but did not think that the colonial subjects would be willing to pay a municipal tax to fund the provision of street lights. The people were so fearful of that tax, he noted, that the "majority of... [them] would prefer that the Town should remain in its present state of almost total darkness..."3 The acting governor hoped, however, that the available water power would make possible the introduction of electricity in Lagos "at no very great cost." In December of that year, Governor Carter stated in a correspondence to the Secretary of State that the "question of efficiently lighting the town of Lagos has become one of great importance, and if it is financially practicable I should like to see the electric system introduced."4 Carter proposed to install 120 lamps across the city at intervals of 220 feet to 220 yards. He also suggested that the current in the lagoon, which often ran at about three knots, might be harnessed to generate electricity for use in Lagos.

Proposals for illuminating the streets of Lagos were considered at length in correspondence between Lagos and London. However, it was decided to extend electricity to only a few strategic buildings, the hospital and the Government House. The use of oil to illuminate the two buildings was considered "dangerous, inconvenient and expensive."5 A saving of £39 per annum would be made if electricity replaced kerosene illumination at the hospital. Unfortunately, the introduction of electricity to Lagos made a false start because the wrong equipment was imported from England. The governor declared that such mistakes must be avoided if possible in the case of Lagos "where there is an almost total absence of mechanical appliances and skilled labour."6

Eventually, in 1898, electric street lighting was introduced in Lagos. However, this was limited mainly to the European residential area. Even so, the service did not operate all night as the number of staff in charge of the facility was insufficient to keep it running beyond 11 p.m., after which it was switched off. The cost of running the light all night was put at almost £2,000 per annum. This included the wages of European staff and an increase in the expenditure on coal. The Secretary of State appeared to have endorsed these proposals for, by March 1899, it was noted that the electric light "continues to run all night." Yet, failure by the Secretary of State to sanction additional expenditure would cause a reversion to the practice of switching it off at 11 p.m, ironically at a time when burglars were likely to be most active."7

The question of street lighting and burglaries recurred later in the 1940s when the General Manager of the Shell Company reported "a recent increase in the incidence of burglaries at Ikoyi, particularly at houses owned by this company."8 He called for an increase in the number of police personnel patrolling the streets but emphasized that the absence or malfunctioning of street lights in some streets had made them prone to such criminal activities. The police, however, advanced the theory that the burglaries were inside jobs but acknowledged that "certain parts of Ikoyi are badly lighted... Waring Road is one of the worst which no doubt accounts for it being fairly high on the burglary list."9 The police concluded that, while the incidence of burglaries was not higher than it had been in the past, certain steps had to be taken to check the crime. Consequently, it recommended the following in order of precedence: co-operation by European residents in treating their own servants with suspicion and keeping temptation out of their way; refusing to allow outsiders to live in their compounds or visit at nights; better street lighting; and more police patrols.10 It may be noted that the police recommendations were laced with the racism and colonial paternalism of this era vis-a-vis the colonial peoples. In the aftermath of this, twenty-one extra street lights were installed at Ikoyi at a cost of £45.

Power Generation, Tariffs, Rate Collection, Rationing and Licensing of Generators During the Colonial Period
The Ijora Power Station, formally commissioned in 1923, was the major source of electricity supply to Lagos and environs during the colonial period. At inception, it had a capacity for generating up to 20 megawatts of electricity from steam turbines and coal-fired boilers. It has, however, been constantly upgraded from that time up to the present. By 1943, the city had become "entirely dependent for supply" on the two turbo-alternators in use at Ijora.11 In the late 1940s, a second phase of development was commenced at Ijora. Known as "Ijora B," the plant had a generating capacity of 85 megawatts. The station was oil-fired and this made it the most modern power station in the country. Ijora B was formally commissioned by Queen Elizabeth II of England when she visited Nigeria in 1956. The third stage of construction in the 1960s added 30.2 megawatts of electricity to take the total installed capacity of the station to 142 megawatts. The fourth phase of development at the station witnessed the addition of three new gas turbines in 1978, each with a capacity of 20 megawatts."12

A concomitant of electricity generation and distribution is the cost to the consumer. In general, the charge for electricity consumption in colonial Lagos varied with the *consumer's income and circumstances. However, petitions to the government and newspaper reports of this period suggest that consumers were not always getting the best from the service. A Lagos newspaper captured the situation for the generality of consumers in the late 1920s: "When light was first installed in Lagos the charge per unit was eight pence, now with an enlarged staff and a very big plant, with less illumination the cost is 1/3 per unit."13 This increased charge may have contributed to the high incidence of default in the payment of electricity bills, especially in the context of the prevailing global economic depression. The government resorted to litigation to check this trend, but it was forced to write off many bad debts.*

Ordinarily, a consumer's supply was disconnected if a bill was not settled after seven days of its issuance. In practice, however, "each consumer was allowed roughly five weeks credit instead of seven days allowed by the Ordinance."14 It was not possible in practice to enforce the seven-day ultimatum and the option of extending the period of grace while efforts were made to recover the debts was considered as "economic in operation and satisfactory to the consumer and Department alike."15 However, this was abused by many consumers in Lagos who accumulated debts in excess of £10. The recourse to litigation was also problematic as many of the defaulters absconded or pleaded insolvency. In 1933 and 1934, the government wrote off bad debts amounting to £26.18.1 d and £28.5.2d, respectively.16 It had become glaring that a "great amount of work [was being] done in vain to recover debts of this nature."17 Consequently, the Commissioner of the Colony proposed measures to check the incidence of default which had led to the accumulation of bad debts.

Separate card indexes were to be created for two categories of consumers. One card would be for those "about whose ability to pay their current bills, there could be no reasonable doubt, or who could easily be made to pay if they defaulted." In this group were colonial officials, firms of standing and owners of substantial amounts of property. Persons who could find good sureties for the payment of their bills could also be listed on the first index. The other card index would be for all other consumers. Those would make a reasonable deposit which would, if necessary, be used to pay arrears due from them. The deposit would approximate the value of the current that the consumer was likely to consume within a certain period. Payments by both categories of consumers would be recorded on their cards, which would be checked monthly. Any consumer who was in arrears would be promptly notified to pay up to date. Failure to do this within a specified number of days would result in the disconnection of the premises and the settlement of outstanding bills out of the deposit.

It is not clear from the records whether the Director of Public Works accepted these proposals. But there is evidence that the government continued to take legal action

against defaulters in a vain bid to make them settle their bills. A report of October 1934 captured the fate of this approach: "Legal action was taken against (...) debtors but was unsuccessful. It was reported in Court that (...) the debtors could be found."
18A different dimension to this was the charge for street lighting, which tended to be heavy on well-lit streets. "The present cost of lighting the Yaba Estate streets," it was stated in 1932, "makes further development in this direction prohibitive."19 The annual charge for the 82-watt lamps in use for illuminating the estate was £460, which was approximately half the estimated revenue from rates collected on the estate in the 1932/33 financial year. This placed the management of the estate in a quandary: more street lights were required to keep pace with the rapid growth of the estate; but the "heavy charges" made this impossible. If the electricity charges were reduced to five pence per unit, which would add up to £3.6.8d per lamp per annum, the estate's budget for street lighting (£350) would have been adequate. But the actual charges exceeded this budgetary allocation by £110. Consequently, the request to reduce the charges to five pence per unit (£3.6.8d per 40 watt lamp) from October 1932 was granted.
20The problem was not limited to the Yaba Estate but affected the entire city.

The Lagos Town Council was charged £6,000 per annum in 1924 for street lighting in Lagos at the approximate cost of nine pence per unit. This charge remained in force until 1932 when, to the dismay of Town Council officials, the Electrical Engineer-in-Chief proposed to increase it. The officials opposed any increase in the charge. It was even suggested that the Council reduce the number of street lights in order to cut costs! Finally, it was agreed that the existing charges would be retained but that they would have to be raised in the future. In addition, the intensity of the street lights was to be reduced if street lighting would be extended to more areas of the city.
21The proposal to reduce street lighting was not well received. It was paradoxical that while public funds had been expended on an electric plant at Ebute Metta, "the public of Lagos (was) faced with the fact that they cannot get street lighting because they cannot afford the Electrical Engineer's charges."22 A compromise was to redistribute street lights in the metropolis and to reduce "the extravagant lighting on Carter Bridge." The redistribution was to favour disadvantaged areas on the island, particularly "[badly lit quarters of the Native Town... as most European quarters of the Town are mostly extremely well, and in some parts unnecessarily well, illuminated."23 The distribution of street lights was to take into consideration the requirements of the police and the general public. While police duty demanded "a delicate balance of light and darkness," preference was to be given to "those roads most frequented and inhabited."
24In general, though electricity was supplied to a growing number of people in Lagos throughout the twentieth century, its use was subjected to restrictions, such as rationing. This became inevitable when the number of consumers increased and the demand for electricity exceeded the supply. In addition to normal shortfalls in the supply,

there was a specific instance when a delay in the delivery of materials from the United Kingdom incapacitated the Lagos electricity supply system.25 Therefore, regulations were introduced which, among others, placed restrictions on the use of electrical appliances. The restrictions, which applied to Ikoyi, Lagos, Ebute Metta and Yaba, where the bulk of the consumers lived, were as follows:

No reconnections will be made to residential premises disconnected prior to 1st January 1947.
The premises of consumers disconnected for non-payment will not be reconnected.
No extensions of any installation will be allowed except where these are restricted to off -peak periods or in very special cases where a corresponding amount of load is disconnected in other premises, or where no substitutes for electricity can be provided and the premises cannot be brought into use without a supply, or where the premises provide badly needed facilities for the general public.
No permits will be issued for heating, cooking or other similar apparatus which is not restricted to off-peak use.
Applications for supply to new installations, where these can be connected, will be restricted to minimum lighting requirements only, or to industrial and commercial load for use during the off-peak period.
No permits will be issued for temporary illumination.
Consumers were urged to obviate further restrictions by economizing the use of electricity at all times, especially during the peak load period between 6 p.m. and 10 p.m. They were enjoined to refrain from using cookers, kettles, irons or other heating apparatus during that period. Consumers were not to switch on any more lights or fans than were necessary at any time. All water heaters were to be switched off during the peak period and defaulters were threatened with disconnection. The restrictions were to be in place for several months if consumers complied with the instructions.

The above account clearly indicates that there was already a discernible gap between rising demand and power generating capacity in Lagos during the late colonial period. Meanwhile, the Electricity Corporation of Nigeria (ECN), established under Nigerian Ordinance No. 1 of 1950, was saddled with the responsibility of generating and distributing electric power. It was described as "an autonomous commercial enterprise in a monopolistic setting."26 The virtual monopoly of ECN, conferred sweeping powers on it and made it immune from sanction or liability for damage or loss sustained by any consumer on account of the interruption of its supplies.

Private power generation by states, firms and individuals was, however, permitted by licence. This required the operator of a plant to generate electricity not exceeding ten kilowatts for domestic purposes and up to a limit of 200 kilowatts for industrial purposes. A fee of £2.2.0d was payable on the issuance of a licence *for any installation up to and including 100 kilowatts installed capacity. Furthermore, the plant would be installed for the sole purpose of generating electricity for the owner's use and not for sale. The* licence *was valid only as long as the public supply of electricity was not available; the power plant would cease to operate as soon as the public supply was restored. No compensation was to be paid for the suspension of the plant.27*

The Federal Government, however, licensed *the Nigeria Electricity Supply Company (NESCO) to operate hydro-electric power stations to generate electric power for the tin mining community on the Jos Plateau. The company also sold energy to the E. C .N. for distribution to private consumers in Jos, Bukuru and Vom. The African Timber and Plywood Company Limited at Sapele and the Shell Petroleum Development Company of Nigeria in the Niger Delta were also licensed to generate electricity. The comparative generating capacity of the different energy producers are detailed in the following table, which clearly indicates that the E.C.N, alone accounted for over 80 per cent of the total output.*

With regard to Lagos, several industrial and commercial concerns applied for license to operate various types of electricity generating plants. West African Fisheries and Cold Storage, for example, applied for a licence in June 1950 to install two 40-kilowatt generating sets "as a standby against breakdown of local electricity supply" and for the firm "to maintain continuous power supply."28 Although several firms secured the licences to operate their own generating plants, they criticized the clause in the agreement which limited the licence to the periods when the public supply failed. But as the chief electrical engineer admitted, "[present indications are that the Corporation will not be embarrassed by demands for a supply of electricity at all Undertakings, for some years to come."29

By May 1951, six licences had been issued to five firms: The Amalgamated Engineering Company Limited; Pauling and Company Limited; A.G. Leventis and Company Limited; The Colonial Development Corporation (W.A.) Limited; and The West African Publicity Limited. The licences permitted them to install generating plants of various models and capacity in their respective workshops and premises.30 The number of licensees *increased to eight in 1958, with the addition of the Ikorodu Ceramic Industries and Barclays Bank. Nevertheless, the usage of generators was severely limited to big commercial and industrial concerns and such efforts at private power generation merely supplemented the supply by the E.C.N. It may be concluded that power supply was coming under some strain towards the end of the colonial era; but the situation did not reach crisis proportions, as was to be the case from the mid-1960s. Already, private power generation under licence was becoming fashionable, although only industrial establishments applied for such licences. This contrasted with developments in subsequent decades when generators of all capacities were acquired by private consumers in the face of perennial shortages.*

The Post-Independence Era, the 1960s to 2000

The situation outlined above persisted till the mid-1960s, when the power supply situation began to deteriorate considerably, leading to severe shortages. Olukoju continues:

> *"The years 1965 and 1966," it has been noted, "were among the worst years of power shortage crisis in [pre-civil war] Nigeria."31 In the Lagos area, scheduled power cuts in 1965 alone occurred 105 times and totalled 97 hours. This was caused by a combination of factors, mainly technical and managerial.32 The General Manager of the E.C.N., Mr. Y. Sun, explained that the largest turbine at the Ijora Power Station C had been defective since 1963. A second roll blade was damaged in 1965 but bad welding when installing new blades caused a reduction in the plant's generating capacity. In addition, a delay in the commissioning of the new 17,000 kilowatt (KW) plant, a shipping strike in England and a burst boiler at the Ijora Station (which caused a considerable loss of water) compounded the problem.*

> *Compared to the crisis situation of the period 1980-2002, this was mere child's play; but in the conditions of the 1960s, the unstable electric power supply was unsettling. In any case, there was already a widening gap between demand and supply in the electric power sector. The total installed capacity in the entire country increased by some 82 per cent between 1960 and 1966, whereas the total demand increased by about 215 per cent, owing to an "increasing rate of industrialization."33 The rising demand for electricity meant that power plants had to be kept running without sufficient routine maintenance and repairs. The resultant breakdown of equipment, cable faults, mechanical fatigue and the inefficiency of maintenance engineers contributed to making power failures in Lagos more frequent in the late 1960s. There was, therefore, a recourse to load shedding of the magnitude of over 800,000 KWH between January and December 1966 alone in metropolitan Lagos. Each load shedding lasted about an hour.34 The economic consequences of the frequent load shedding in the Greater Lagos area have been noted as follows:*

[One] consequence of power failures was dislocation in production programmes of majority of firms… [Most] firms, unable to meet some orders either deferred or cancelled them. This caused scarcity of such items as cement, beer, soft drinks, textiles, motor and cycle tyres and food products with the resultant price inflation… Inflation in Lagos area was spread to other areas of the country since Lagos was and remains the industrial/commercial hub of Nigeria.35

Conditions changed for the better from 1967/68 to 1971/ 72 following the commissioning of the Kainji Dam hydroelectric project. But demand soon overwhelmed supply in spite of the establishment, by decree in 1972, of the National Electric Power Authority (NEPA). The situation became so critical in 1974 that NEPA had to reactivate some thermal plants which had been phased out when the Kainji hydroelectric project came into operation.36

In effect, despite its monopoly of power supply, NEPA failed to meet the demands of consumers, particularly in Lagos. On 20 May 1975, two of the four power stations at Kainji broke down and defied efforts to repair them. This plunged the entire nation into crisis, as many industries (the vast majority of which were in Lagos) simply ground to a halt.37This was a foretaste of what would happen in the 1990s and beyond. The following observations about the power supply situation in Nigeria up to 1975 are very revealing:

> *The power system in Nigeria has been in frequent power shortage crisis since (the) early 1960's up to the present. The relief brought by Kainji (First phase) was very temporary, as the capacity of 320 MW was "oversubscribed" in a matter of months by the electric energy hungry consumers. The investment policy of NEPA as to size and timing of power projects has therefore been suboptimal. The net effect has been a continuous pressure of demand on capacity leading to plant breakdowns and consequently a power shortage. The solution calls for an increase in generating capacity with larger generating units.38*

The above comments might as well have been made in 1999 or 2001, given their continuing relevance.
By the mid-1980s, power supply in Nigeria, particularly in Lagos, was so erratic that NEPA was derided as "Never Expect Power Always."39 This was in view of its failure to meet the stupendous rise in the demand for electricity as indicated in the table below. The number of residential consumers had increased by more than 500 per cent between 1970 and 1987, while consumption had increased eleven times within the same period. The situation reached crisis proportions in

the 1990s: entire neighbourhoods could be in complete darkness for months; the more fortunate wards or streets had to put up with "load-shedding," by which power was rationed to different streets and neighbourhoods at the whims of officials. It is worth stressing that the crisis of the late twentieth century was a culmination of years of neglect or of wrong policies.

Coupled with the great shortfall in power generation has been the problem of distribution. It is generally agreed that this is a major problem that NEPA has not been able to solve. To be fair, many consumers engage in illegal connection, often with the connivance of serving or former employees of NEPA. Moreover, electric cables and poles are routinely damaged by bush burning, domestic fire incidents, rainstorms or vehicle accidents, or stolen by criminals. The costs of replacement generally give rise to delays in effecting repairs and thus prolong the resultant power cuts.

In addition, NEPA's policy on the maintenance and replacement of equipment was faulty and remains so. It failed to appreciate that it required four to five years to order, install and commission new plants and that some "lead time" ought to have been allowed for their purchase and installation. In other words, as soon as the Kainji project was commissioned, immediate orders should have been placed for additional equipment in anticipation of wear and tear of the functional ones. Waiting for them to break down before placing orders would, therefore, create a time lag with predictable consequences.40 Furthermore, the organization itself has come to be associated with inefficiency and corruption. Inefficient debt collection, mismanagement of funds, sabotage of equipment by vandals within and outside NEPA, fluctuating water levels at Kainji, and a host of other factors have compounded the Authority's dismal record. These factors are weighty and require some elaboration.

With regard to the vandalization of NEPA equipment, two professors of Electrical Engineering lamented that they did not know of any other country in the world, apart from Nigeria, where public property and infrastructural facilities were vandalized. While conceding that NEPA had other problems, they lamented the attitude of Nigerians to public property, especially NEPA equipment and installations, a major contribution to its woes. This phenomenon is worrisome and has defied solution. The crime has often been perpetrated directly by serving or retired NEPA employees acting alone or in connivance with others. Vandalization thus reflects a lack of patriotism and attachment to the Nigerian state, the absence of an effective system of sanctions, as well as a national culture of greed and mindless accumulation of wealth.

NEPA's dismal record of debt collection is aggravated by the fact that its greatest debtors are government agencies. The Federal, State and Local Government agencies and functionaries, including the military and para-military establishments, have accumulated huge debts running into billions of naira. Attempts to recover such sums of money have been frustrated by the predatory culture of military rule, when the defaulters accumulated debts with impunity. However, unlike the practice during the colonial period, NEPA has not explored the possibility of litigation to recover its debts.

Mismanagement of funds has been a longstanding feature of the operations of NEPA, like those of other state-owned enterprises in post-independence Nigeria. Regardless of wild fluctuations in the exchange rate and the precipitous fall in the value of the naira, it is clear from the table below that since the era of military rule huge sums of money have been voted in the Federal Government's annual budgets for capital and recurrent expenditure by NEPA. However, startling revelations from investigations into the activities of high echelon government officials in the Ministries of Power and Steel since the 1970s indicate that most of the funds were never expended as budgeted. Large scale fraud has come to be associated with the energy sector (with the Second Republic Ministry of Steel achieving notoriety as the "Ministry of Steal"!). However, it can also be seen from the table that the greatest outlays were made between 1999 and 2002, albeit when the naira had declined against the US dollar. Whatever impact these will make may not be immediate, given the "time lag" element in such investments.

NEPA's woes have been compounded by its worsening debt portfolio. The Vice President of Nigeria, Atiku Abubakar, confirmed that the Authority was carrying a liability of N40 billion, made up of unpaid loans, accumulated pensions, power purchase liabilities and inter-governmental cross debts.42 This situation has placed NEPA in a most precarious financial position: it is not generating enough funds, owing to poor revenue collection and monumental fraud, and it is caught in a debt trap. Either way it cannot generate or distribute electricity to satisfy the demand of its customers.

The failure of NEPA to meet the energy requirements of its customers has naturally compelled electricity consumers to resort to various schemes of self-help, such as the use of generators, candles and hurricane lanterns, the importation of which experienced a boom.

Although precise figures of importation and distribution in the Lagos area are not readily available, it is clear that several thousand homes had to depend on one or another of these substitutes for NEPA. The use of candles and hurricane lanterns in homes where petrol had been stored during the perennial petrol shortages of the 1990s caused fire outbreaks, leading to the loss of lives and property. One such fire incidents at Badiya (Ijora) in 1989, caused by a candle, damaged NEPA equipment to the tune of N5 million and plunged many parts of the city into darkness.43

Industrial establishments in Lagos have had to operate far below their installed capacities because of the huge shortfall in the power supply. Many industrial enterprises either closed down or relied heavily on power generating units. This raised production costs, which were reflected in the higher prices of local compared to foreign manufactures. Since many of the factories operated below installed capacity, they had to lay off their staff. This had grave social and economic consequences. Many artisanal or small scale enterprises depend on a regular power supply. A large number of these have been forced to fold up. In this category are the barbing/hairdressing, tailoring or fashion designing, welding, panel-beating, electrical and electronics repair enterprises. Not only were the proprietors, employees and apprentices engaged in these enterprises thrown into the labour market, some have taken to crime in desperation. The spate of violent robberies in the late 1990s derived from the high rate of unemployment generated by power shortages.

Consequently, though other parts of Nigeria suffered proportionately, Lagos was worst hit because it contains almost 60 per cent of the country's industrial establishments and consumes about half of the electric power generated by both official and private means. The attempt by the Lagos State government to enlist the support of independent power generators initially raised hopes but soon generated anxiety when the US giant, Enron, which had been contracted to supplement supply by NEPA, went bankrupt.44 However, a solution was found when another firm took over Enron's power generating enterprise in Lagos and succeeded in generating power for industrial enterprises. Though this has added to the total generating capacity, it has made little difference, given the rising demand for electricity in Lagos in particular. In any case, the cost of generation and distribution is higher than NEPA's but the entire experiment in independent power production gives hope that much could still be achieved in this direction given the right conditions. For now, it seems that Lagos will continue to experience load-shedding and regular blackouts in the foreseeable future."

Nigerians were jubilant and thought that things were really going to change, when in 2013, the Jonathan Goodluck Administration announced the eventual privatization of NEPA, which transformed into Power Holding Company of Nigeria (PHCN). Ironically, the sham which was called privatization was primarily a sale of government asset to government cronies and shenanigans.

Things have remained virtually the same, if not aggravated. The Generating companies (GENCOs) and Distribution companies (DISCOs) have found it hard to keep their head above the water. Consequently, power production and supply still hovers around 5000MW for 200 million people.

Yet, it seems that the foolhardiness of government is inexhaustible, as the power sector continues to go through one upheaval after another. On the 4th of Sep 2017, the *Daily Trust* reported the following:

> *The National Executive Council of Trade Union Congress of Nigeria (TUC) has condemned the provision of N39 billion to privatized electricity distribution companies, saying the move by the Federal Government is against its privatization policy. The union, in a communiqué at the end of its meeting in Lagos, considered the pronouncement by the Minister of Power, Works and Housing, Babatunde Fashola, in Kano that government would give loans to the Distribution Companies (DISCOs) to meet electricity meter supply as a contradiction of privatization policy.*
>
> *The minister was quoted to have said the fund was meant to help the distribution companies bridge over 10 million metering gap in ensuring uninterrupted power generation and distribution. But the union demanded that government should not use public funds to fund private businesses or alternatively, reverse the privatization of the power sector as a failed policy. It also frowned at the Public Private Partnership being implemented in the health sector which it noted, has deviated from the original blue print of the 2004 working document, indicating that the critical health sector is now being commercialised. TUC warned that the consequence was that common Nigerians would be deprived of health care services. The union also expressed concern over the lip service on the patronage of Made-in-Nigeria goods, condemning the use of foreign materials by government agencies such as the military and paramilitary.*

The announcement to give loans to DISCOs greatly shocked everyone, to put it mildly, seeing that the very essence of privatization had been nullified. The Power Minister once argued at a forum organized by the French consulate that power provision is not directly proportional to economic growth stating that when the economy was growing at 7 percent, Nigeria produced less than 5000MW, which is its present output yet the economy is not growing. The scorn was palpable.

Again, it was reported by the Vanguard on the 12th of Oct 2017 that,

The Federal Government has commenced negotiations with operators of the Electricity Distribution Companies DISCOs) with a view to ceding some of their shares to accommodate new investors who would bring in more funds to increase their service delivery.
The Minister of State for Budget and National Planning, Mrs. Zainab Mohammed, disclosed this at the end of the Nigeria Economic Summit 23#, in Abuja, Thursday.

Power is by far the most strategic sub-sector in the Nigerian economy. Reports have it that Nigeria has an energy deficit of some 23,000 megawatts, which is costing the economy about $1.3 billion a year. Its average per capita energy consumption stands at 129 kilowatt hours compared with 491 kW in India and 12,607 kW in the United States. Nigeria spends about $13 billion a year in diesel-generated power when it would only require about $10 billion a year each year for the next few years to help the country meet the dream of joining the world's 20 biggest economies by 2020. The sector needs immediate $15-20 billion of investment in the next three years. It is estimated that addressing this gap could add about two per cent to the nation's Gross Domestic Product.

A report by the Socio-Economic Rights and Accountability Project (SERAP) titled *From Darkness to Darkness: How Nigerians are Paying the Price for Corruption in the Electricity Sector* shed more light on the issues assailing the power sector as reported by Vanguard newspaper:

> The report presented to the media, by Yemi Oke, Ass. Professor, Energy/Electricity Law, Faculty of Law, University of Lagos discloses that "the country has lost more megawatts in the post-privatization era due to corruption, impunity, among other social challenges reflected in the report."

> The report shows that, "The much-publicized power sector reforms in Nigeria under the Electric Power Sector Reform Act of 2005 is yet to yield desired and/or anticipated fruits largely due to corruption and impunity of perpetrators, regulatory lapses and policy inconsistencies. Ordinary Nigerians continue to pay the price for corruption in the electricity sector–staying in darkness, but still made to pay crazy electricity bills."

> Mr. Femi Falana SAN who chaired the report launch said that, "This report is a must read, and I promise to lead in the follow-up litigation efforts to ensure the full implementation of the recommendations of the report."

> The report launch was also attended by Babatunde Irukera, the Director General/Chief Executive of the Consumer Protection Council (CPC); and Mr.

Ibrahim Magu, Chairman Economic and Financial Crimes Commission (EFCC) who was represented by Mr. Osita Nwajah, Director, Public Affairs EFCC. Both promised to work to ensure the full implementation of the recommendations contained in the report.

The report accuses the Dr. Ransom Owan-led board of the Nigerian Electricity Regulatory Commission (NERC) of allegedly "settling officials with millions of Naira as severance packages and for embarrassing them with alleged Three Billion Naira (N3,000,000,000.00) fraud. The authorities must undertake a thorough, impartial and transparent investigation as to the reasons why corruption charges were withdrawn, and to recover any corrupt funds."

The report also called for the reopening and effective prosecution of corruption allegations, including the alleged "looting of the benefits of families of the deceased employees of Power Holding Company of Nigeria (PHCN)" levelled against a former Permanent Secretary in the Ministry of Power, Godknows Igali."

The report reads:

> "The Obasanjo's administration spent $10 billion on NIPP with no results in terms of increase in power generation. $13.278,937,409.94 was expended on the power sector in eight years while unfunded commitments amounted to $12 billion.

> "The Federal Government then budgeted a whopping N16 billion for the various reforms under Liyel Imoke (2003 to 2007) which went down the drains as it failed to generate the needed amount of electricity or meet the set goals. Imoke was alleged to have personally collected the sum of $7.8 million for the execution of the contract for the construction of the Jos-Yola Transmission Line, which was never executed. There were documented/reported allegations of corruption against Imoke that fizzled-out shortly thereafter.

> "Professor Chinedu Nebo handed over the assets of the PHCN to private investors on November 1, 2013. Prof. Nebo is alleged to have corruptly funded the privatized power sector with over N200 Billion despite privatization. The allegation of N200 Billion funding of the privatized power sector during Prof Nebo's tenure should be thoroughly and transparently investigated and anyone suspected to be responsible prosecuted. Any corrupt funds should be fully recovered.

"Our research revealed that the sum of N1.5 billion with which the vehicles were acquired was allegedly sourced from the diverted N27 billion insurance premium of deceased workers of the defunct Power Holding Company of Nigeria (PHCN).

"The National Assembly and members should desist from and avoid manipulating the award of electricity contracts or cite projects in their constituencies under the guise of "Constituency Project". The National Assembly should publish and ensure the full implementation of the recommendations of all power-related investigations to date.

"The Federal Government should back-down from Rural Electrification initiatives and allow States to undertake rural electrification through their respective Local Governments and Development Areas. Federal Government should consider fully divesting its stakes in the power sector and allow for efficient, decentralized sector governance by Federal and State governments, as appropriate, in line with the provisions of the Second Schedule, paragraph 13 and 14 of the Constitution of the Federal Republic of Nigeria 1999 (as amended).

"The 36 state governments should wake up to their rights, duties and obligations under the Constitution of the Federal Republic of Nigeria relating to the power sector by working to promote and ensure access to regular and uninterrupted electricity supply for all residents within their states. The 36 state governments have been abdicating the duties to the power sector, bearing in mind that Power is an item on the Concurrent Legislative List under the Nigerian Constitution 1999 (as amended).

"When the late Bola Ige took up the mantle of the Power and Steel Ministry in 1999, he probably didn't understand the magnitude of problems in the power sector and consequently, promised that within six months of his appointment, "power failure will be a thing of the past" and that on a regular basis, he will brief the nation on the state of power, steel and aluminum. Current minister Babatunde Fashola SAN also claimed that 'a serious Government will fix the power problem in six months.'
"The power sector under Ige was characterized by epileptic and unreliable supply, bogus billing and archaic rate collection. The late Minister failed and was unable to put an end to these. His failure was attributed to acts of sabotage and corruption by people who were benefitting from the use of

generators. The late Bola Ige was not accused of corruption.

"When Rilwan Lanre Babalola (2008 to 2010) took over the affairs in the Ministry of Power, he met 3,700MW on ground and promised to increase it to 6,000MW and ensure a 24-hour power supply by the end of 2009. Six months after assuring Nigerians of making a significant impact in the sector, in September 2009, the 3,700MW capacity he met on ground dropped to 2,710MW which shortfall was attributed to inadequate supply of gas to the new generators.

"The duo, Elumelu and Ugbane allegedly colluded in misappropriating over N10 billion public funds from the account of Rural Electrification Agency (REA). The research also established, based on evaluation and analyzing documents, a prima-facie case of misappropriation of unspent funds at the end of the year instead of returning same to the treasury. Alleged misappropriation of N500million to buy houses; diversion of REA's funds; flouting of government's rules on award of contracts and award of fictitious and unnecessary contracts without following due process.

"The government of Nigeria handed over the transmission company to a Canadian company Manitoba, to manage and under a management service contract of over $200 million. Findings also show that the Transmission Company of Nigeria could not execute most of its approved 44 projects after having 50 percent of its N30 billion 2016 budget released to it. Funds were released from Eurobond. $23.6 million allegedly paid to Manitoba Hydro International (MHI) of Canada to manage the Transmission Company of Nigeria (TCN) would appear to be without due process.

"The privatization of PHCN would appear to have yielded the country total darkness. Gains of privatization were lost through alleged corruption, manipulation of rules and disregard to extant laws and lack of transparency in the exercise. The PBE encouraged the deferment of payment and restructuring of payment terms in contravention of bidding rules to the disadvantage of other bidders.

"Billing methodology shrouded in secrecy. Billings do not reflect actual electricity consumptions in most cases. Most if not all, officials of the DISCOs are still very corrupt and demand gratification from customers before doing the job they are paid to do. Grand corruption against the

Federal Government owner of the 40% stakes in the DISCOS, and by implications, the Nigerian masses due to non-remittance or under-remittances of the monies collected by the DISCOs.

"The Manitoba deal is shrouded in secrecy as essential details of the deal remain unknown to Nigerians till date. The authorities should undertake a public-oriented audit on the state of affairs of the TCN two years before and after the Manitoba deal. The outcome of the audit should form basis for further action and charges in court against the suspected perpetrators and corrupt funds fully recovered.

"The Federal Government should undertake a thorough, impartial and transparent investigation into the power sector privatization with a view to doing things the right, fair and just way. Ownership of public stakes of 40% in those entities should be revisited and further privatized to avoid using government/public resources to subsidize private entities.

"Attention should be focused also on petty corruption. Petty corruption in the electricity sector has not received much attention, as the focus has been on grand corruption in the sector.

"The Attorney-General of the Federation and Minister of Justice Abubakar Malami SAN should request the report of the House of Representative Committee that probed government spending in the power sector from 2000 to 2007, and the Elumelu House Probe Committee which had accused 21 persons and 36 companies of subversion of government policy on due process make the report public and ensure appropriate legal action against anyone suspected to be involved in corruption as well as full recovery of corrupt funds.

"Undocumented, monumental fraud and corruption is said to be perpetrated at the Niger Delta Power Holding Company (NDPHC) and investigation by the EFCC and ICPC will ensure that those involved are effectively brought to justice.

"Mr. Malami should direct the EFCC and ICPC to probe metering and billing fraud and corruption and bribery among Discos. Most consumers are unhappy will their billing methodology and feel short-changed by the operators. Mr Malami should promptly make progress on all outstanding cases of corruption in the electricity sector including by ensuring effective prosecution of all power sector cases being handled by the Ministry.

"The ICPC should make public the status of the investigation and recommendations for prosecution (if any) on the AEDC Recruitment Scandal/Jumbo Pay Scandal given the facts that the Nigerian Government and public have 40% stakes in the AEDC. The Manitoba deal is shrouded in secrecy as essential details of the deal remain unknown to Nigerians till date. The EFCC/ICPC should lead a public-oriented audit on the state of affairs of the TCN two years before and after the Manitoba deal.

"The ICPC should tell Nigerians about the current status of the probe of the recruitment scandal and corruption-induced jumbo pay to workers of the Abuja Electricity Distribution Company (AEDC Plc). Anyone found to be responsible should be brought to justice and corrupt funds fully recovered."

Notwithstanding the myriad problems confronting the power sector, Nigerians remain hopeful that someday there will be light at the end of the tunnel.

Transportation Infrastructure

Nigeria has developed an extensive national network of roads and bridges. Nigeria's roads carry more than 90% of domestic passengers and freight. Road network density is more than double that of other resource-rich African countries, although still only half of the levels found in Africa's middle-income countries. Few areas remain unconnected to national backbones, and are largely concentrated in the central, western and eastern parts of the country.
The country's regional connections are fair, with a number of transnational corridors. These include connections to neighbouring countries like Niger, Chad, Cameroon and Benin, as well as coastal roads joining routes to Dakar in Senegal or Abidjan in Cote d'Ivoire.
The Trans-Sahara Highway connects Nigeria with Algeria via Niger. A cross-African route, the Lagos-Mombasa Highway, links Nigeria, Cameroon, the Central African Republic, the DRC, and Uganda. (PWC publication - Nigerian roads and connectivity)

The deplorable state and quality of roads in Nigeria has certainly become a national shame and a monumental embarrassment as there is hardly any part of the country that can boast of good, motorable roads, be they roads in Trunk A (federal), Trunk B (state) or Trunk C (local government). As a result of poor leadership and woeful planning, there are no tangible alternatives either. The railway system is dysfunctional while the air transport sector is an arena of inefficiency and a cesspool of corruption. With an estimated 193,200km of roads in the country and the Federal Government in charge of about 34,000km, leaving the rest to the states and local governments, unfortunately, no tier of government can be said to have acquitted itself creditably on matters of roads construction and maintenance. Scores of innocent people are killed daily in avoidable accidents on account of the bad roads. Man-hours are lost in traffic. And the national economy suffers incalculable losses. It is high time governments at all levels treated road infrastructure as priority to enhance economic development and also see it as a national security tool.

Since 1999, a whopping N1.4 trillion ($8.5 billion) has reportedly been spent on road construction or maintenance with very little evidence of the money spent. The system is rotten and merely serves as a veritable platform for corruption.
In the 2015 budget, the Federal Government supposedly slashed the Works' Ministry's budget from N100 billion to N11 billion, which many criticized as a minus for roads maintenance. But even at that, N11 billion could have made a sizable difference, if the fund was judiciously utilized.

With no functional railway system, roads are the only means of movement of people and goods - meaning that the nation's economy is grounded with such bad roads as Nigeria has. Some of the worst highways include the Lagos-Ibadan Expressway, Shagamu-Ore, Onitsha-Enugu−Port Harcourt road, Ikorodu-Shagamu road, Okene-Lokoja-Abuja and Rijau-Kontagora road in Niger State. With a few exceptions, indeed, virtually all the highways in the country are in a terrible state. It is needless to mention the majority of Trunk B roads which have barely received any attention.

Travelling through most Nigerian roads, especially, during the rainy season is hellish. Vehicles break down; heavy-duty trucks get stuck in mud and overturn. Motorists disembark at such horrible spots to push crippled vehicles. The result is traffic gridlock on both sides of what seems like a jungle and loss of many lives. 58 years after independence, it is indeed a shame that Nigeria, despite the huge revenue earnings from oil, has yet to develop a good transportation system. Between 2008 and June 2014 alone, Nigeria reportedly earned N44.655 trillion. It is pertinent to ask what premium government places on roads as economic assets which should ordinarily aid national productivity!

There are very few African countries with Nigeria's shameful status with regard to roads. The Lagos-Badagry highway, for example, which links Nigeria with the Republic of Benin, underscores this. Whereas the Nigerian side of what should be a super highway, linking the whole of West Africa, is dilapidated and impassable, the Republic of Benin portion is not only in good condition, it advertises a certain irresponsibility on the part of Nigeria.

In every respect, the Nigerian authorities are guilty. The building of concrete roads with cement, especially, in the southern states where erosion is rife has been canvassed by experts as a solution to the poor durability of asphalt roads. But it seems corruption and a certain insensitivity to the economic well-being of Nigeria prevent those in power from heeding this call. Such corruption, of course, explains a situation in which roads in Nigeria are built at prohibitive costs. Whereas, the World Bank's benchmark for building a kilometre of road is N238 million, the same one-kilometre is built for about N1 billion in Nigeria.

The structure of road ownership and maintenance has always been a thorny issue. The policy

that the three tiers of government have responsibility for roads development and maintenance is in place but flawed in execution. No tier of government consistently maintains its own share of the roads leading to overlapping of duties, conflicts and, eventually, neglect.
This has brought the issue of the flawed federalism Nigeria operates to the fore and for as long as the denial of this error continues, so will irresponsibility in governance.

While the debate rages over who should take responsibility for the roads within a state even when they are supposedly federal, the people, as well as the economy, suffer. Many would claim that job of the Federal Government should be in setting standards, especially, for inter-state highways while the states should have the capacity to bear the responsibility for roads construction and maintenance. In actual fact, neither tier is being judicious with the allocations intended for the development of these infrastructures.
The stark truth is that the decay in infrastructural development in Nigeria has been a tale of chronic weak will and chronically weak leadership.

As Daron Acemoglu and James Robinson have convincingly pointed to the world, in *Why Nations Fail*, that though economic institutions are imperative for determining a country's poverty or prosperity, it is the political institutions that determine what type of economic institutions it will have and how those institutions will function.

<h2 style="text-align:center">Chapter 5</h2>

<h2 style="text-align:center">The Economy and Corruption Hegemony</h2>

The Economy

In 2014, following a rebasing of the country's economic production statistics, Nigeria became the largest economy in sub-Saharan Africa (after nearly 25 years), with a GDP of $510 billion, displacing South Africa to second place ($384 billion) -with a population of 170 million people, and a per capita income of $2,992.

Nigeria ranks 32nd in the world in terms of land mass. This mammoth landmass harbors abundant physical and natural resources. Endowed with about 34 different types of solid minerals in commercial quantities, in about 450 locations spread across the regions, these profuse and significant reserves of solid minerals remain largely untapped and undeveloped.

Nationwide, modern and traditional economic activities exist alongside each other. In the agricultural sector, traditional subsistence farming accounts for over 90 per cent of the production, with the remainder being large-scale modern agribusinesses. A large number of small, informal enterprises and a few modern firms make up the industrial sector, while formal and informal financial institutions co-exist in the financial sector.

Sadly, Nigeria's economic performance has been lack-luster, relative to the country's endowments. Its performance in comparison to its potential has left external observers – and Nigerians – befuddled as to why the country has so far been unable to become a true economic powerhouse. About 60 per cent of Nigerians live below the international poverty level of $1.25 a day in income. Other emerging economies such as Malaysia, South Korea, China and India, which were behind or at the same levels of industrial production in the 1960s and 1970s have transformed their economies and become major players in the world economy, creating a new paradigm of global economic multipolarism. Between 2005 and 2010, the average growth in industrial production for China, India, Brazil and Malaysia was 16.0, 8.0, 3.6, and 2.5 per cent respectively, while Nigeria recorded 2.1 per cent.

- **Agriculture**

In Agriculture, Nigeria ranks sixth worldwide and first in Africa in farm output. The sector accounts for about 18% of GDP and almost one-third of its employment. Nigeria has 19 million heads of cattle, the largest in Africa. Though Nigeria is no longer a major exporter, due to local consumer boom, it is still a major producer of many agricultural products, including cocoa, groundnuts (peanuts), rubber, and palm oil. Cocoa production, mostly from obsolete varieties and overage trees has increased from around 180,000 tons annually to 350,000 tons.

Other major agricultural products include cassava (tapioca), corn, millet, rice, sorghum, and yams. In 2003, livestock production, in order of metric tonnage featured eggs, milk, beef and veal, poultry, and pork, respectively. In the same year, the total fishing catch was 505.8 metric tons. Roundwood removals totaled slightly less than 70 million cubic meters, and sawnwood production was estimated at 2 million cubic meters.

Unarguably, the agricultural sector suffers from extremely low productivity, due to heavy reliance on antiquated methods. Agriculture has failed to keep pace with Nigeria's rapid population growth, so that the country, which once exported food, now imports a significant amount of food to sustain itself.

But in recent times, the story is gradually changing as the government is giving incentives to farm exports, banned importation of the staple, rice, which has led to the cultivation of local rice across the nation as well as encouraging local farm businesses – poultry, snailery, piggery etc.

- **Crude Oil**

Again, Nigeria is the sixth largest producer of crude oil and also has the sixth largest gas reserves in the world. So central to Nigeria's economic profile is the oil and gas sector that it currently accounts for 14.4 per cent of GDP, 90 per cent of the country's total export receipts, and about 80 per cent of total revenue.

Nigeria's proven oil reserves are estimated to be 35 billion barrels (5.6×109 m3); natural gas reserves are well over 100 trillion cubic feet (2,800 km3). Nigeria is a member of the Organization of Petroleum Exporting Countries (OPEC). The types of crude oil exported by Nigeria are Bonny light oil, Forcados crude oil, Qua Ibo crude oil and Brass River crude oil. Poor corporate relations with indigenous communities, vandalism of oil infrastructure, severe ecological damage, and security problems throughout the Niger Delta oil-producing region continue to plague Nigeria's oil sector.

To curb these troubles, the Niger Delta Development Commission (NDDC) was created in order to catalyze economic and social development in the region. Unfortunately, it has become a scam. There are claims that the commission has only benefited cronies of political bigwigs, coupled with allegations of massive corruption.

The U.S. remains Nigeria's largest buyer of crude oil, accounting for 40% of the country's total oil exports; Nigeria provides about 10% of overall U.S. oil imports and ranks as the fifth-largest source for U.S. imported oil.
The United Kingdom is Nigeria's largest trading partner followed by the United States. Although the trade balance overwhelmingly favors Nigeria, thanks to oil exports, a large portion of U.S. exports to Nigeria is believed to enter the country outside of the Nigerian government's official statistics, due to importers seeking to avoid Nigeria's tariffs. To counter smuggling and under-invoicing by importers, in May 2001, the Nigerian government instituted a full inspection program for all imports, and enforcement has been sustained.
The stock of U.S. investment is nearly $7 billion, mostly in the energy sector. Significant exports of liquefied natural gas started in late 1999. (Wikipedia – Nigeria – economy)

Since its return to democracy, Nigeria's oil-dependent economy has been a slippery slope under which we had a windfall in 2015 with prices reaching over $100 per barrel. This led to the creation of the *Sovereign Wealth Fund*, which regrettably, has also been politicized.

- **Industry**

At independence in 1960 and for much of that decade, agriculture was the mainstay of the
Nigerian economy - providing food and employment for the populace, raw materials for the then
nascent industrial sector, and generating the bulk of government revenue and foreign exchange

earnings. Following the discovery of oil and its exploration and exportation in commercial
quantities, the fortunes of agriculture gradually diminished. Crude oil replaced it as the dominant source of revenue and export earnings. This was despite a drive for industrial
development.

The First National Development Plan (1962-68)
Under the First Plan, the country embraced import-substituting industrialization (ISI), with the objective of mobilizing national economic resources and deploying them on a cost/benefit basis among contending projects as a systematic attempt at industrial development.

The period of this plan witnessed the commissioning of energy projects such as the Kainji dam and the Ughelli thermal plants, which provided vital infrastructural backbone for the nascent industrial sector. Other important industrial infrastructure developed during this period, which was considered crucial for catalyzing industrial take-off in Nigeria; included an oil refinery, a development bank, and a mint and security company. Even though the main objective of the ISI strategy was to stimulate the start-up and growth of industries as well as enhance indigenous participation by altering the ownership structure and management of industries, it was characterized by a high degree of technological dependence on foreign know-how to the extent that the domestic factor endowments of the country were grossly neglected.
The focus on an ISI strategy as the cornerstone of industrial development efforts during the period of the First Plan therefore seemed to have neglected many of the factors required for managing the emergent industrial sector and in particular, the management of technologies transferred or acquired.

The Second National Development Plan (1970-74), attempted to address the limitations
of the ISI strategy, and placed emphasis on 'the upgrading of local production of intermediate and
capital goods for sale to other industries'. This was the first systematic effort to create an
industrial structure linked to agriculture, transport, mining, and quarrying. The Second Plan
coincided with Nigeria's newly acquired status as a major petroleum producing country. As the
economy benefited heavily from enormous foreign exchange inflows, the government embraced
ambitious and costly industrial projects in sectors such as iron and steel, cement, salt, sugar,
fertilizer, pulp and paper, among others.

According to the plan, the establishment of industrial projects during this period was inspired by the need to increase the earning power of the populace; minimize social tension by generating more employment; make essential goods easily available; and to

lay the foundation for a self-sustaining economy. The shallow nature of Nigeria's
technological capacity, however, prevented the economy from moving beyond the
elementary phases of these projects, and indeed, virtually all of these projects have
today, either been shut down or operate at very low capacity.
The period of the 1970-74 Plan also witnessed a dramatic shift in policy from private to
public
sector-led industrialization. Industrial planning took place in the public sector which also
executed most of the industrial projects as the government invested directly in
productive
activities. It was clear at this time that Nigerian entrepreneurs did not have the money or
the
techno-managerial capacity to establish and manage such enterprises and so the
government had to lead the way.

On balance, a critical appraisal of the nature of the industrial development challenge of
the 1970s reveals that the limitation was not so much that of finance but dearth of
human capital including techno-managerial capabilities and skills required for initiating,
implementing, and managing industrial projects. This was all the more evident by the
fact that project preparation, feasibility studies, engineering drawings and designs
including construction, erection, and commissioning, relied greatly on foreign technical
skills and services.

The 1972 Act on Indigenization of Enterprises Operating in Nigeria resulted in an
indigenization policy which was subsequently amended, repealed, and replaced by the
Nigerian Enterprises Promotion Act of 1977. The objectives of the policy were to:
• Transfer ownership and control to Nigerians in respect of those enterprises formerly
owned (wholly or partly) and controlled by foreigners;
• Foster widespread ownership of enterprises among Nigerian citizens;
• Create opportunities for Nigerian indigenous businessmen;
• Encourage foreign businessmen and investors to move from the unsophisticated
spheres
of the economy to domains where large investments are required.

The Third National Development Plan (1975-80) was launched at the height of the oil
boom.
Despite a lack of executive capacity in the country, the plan envisaged an investment
outlay of 42 billion NGN (up from 3.2 billion NGN of the Second Plan). Emphasis
remained on public
sector investment in industry, especially heavy industries.
With easy access to foreign exchange, private firms opted for Investments in the light,
low technology consumer industries which were heavily dependent on imported
machinery and raw materials. It became apparent that the country had entered into
industrial project agreements with very little concern for the country and the tail spin
only continued.

The above narrative is Nigeria's attempt since independence at having a cohesive plan to develop her economy.

- ### **Employment Statistics**

Since Q2 2014, Nigeria's economic growth has been decelerating culminating in an economic recession in Q2 2016. The technical indicator of a recession is two consecutive quarters of negative economic growth as measured by a country's gross domestic product (GDP).
The economic recession was technically over in Q2 2017. However, several economic activities are still contracting or recovering sub-optimally.
An economic recession is consistent with an increase in unemployment as jobs are lost and new jobs creation is stalled.
A return to economic growth provides an impetus to employment. However, employment growth may lag, and unemployment rates worsen, especially at the end of a recession, and for many months after.

The unemployment rate, induced by a recession, typically peaks about 15-18 months after the beginning of a recession or 4-8 months after the end of a recession before it returns to its pre-recession trend. This, in the case of Nigeria will be a peak in Q4 2017 which means unemployment will only to return to its normal trend in 2018.

The economically active or working age population (15 – 64 years of age) increased from 110.3 million in Q2 2017 to 111.1 million in Q3 2017.

The labor force population increased from 83.9 million in Q2 2017 to 85.1 million in Q3 2017.
The total number of people in full-time employment (at least 40 hours a week) declined from 52.7 million in Q2 2017 to 51.1 million in Q3 2017 (A loss in full time employed workers may not necessarily be due to job losses. It may also be due to people choosing to work fewer hours hence becoming underemployed or people like intending students or new mothers choosing to leave full time employment entirely or temporarily).
The unemployment rate increased from 14.2% in Q4 2016 to 16.2% in Q2 2017 and 18.8% in Q3 2017.
The number of people within the labor force who are unemployed or underemployed increased from 13.6 million and 17.7 million respectively in Q2 2017, to 15.9 million and 18.0 million in Q3 2017.

Total unemployment and underemployment combined increased from 37.2% in the previous quarter to 40.0% in Q3 2017.
During the quarter Q3 2017, 21.2% of women within the labor force (aged 15-64 and willing, able, and actively seeking work) were unemployed, compared with 16.5% of men within the same period.
In Q3 2017, 16.4% of rural and 23.4% of urban dwellers within the labor force were unemployed and unemployment is increasing at a slightly faster rate for urban dwellers than it is for their rural counterparts.
Underemployment is predominant in the rural areas (26.9% of rural residents within the labor force in Q3 2017), are underemployed (engaged in work for less than 20 hours a week);

compared to 9% of urban residents within the same period.

For the period under review, Q3, 2017, the unemployment rate for young people stood at 33.1% for those aged 15 to 24, and 20.2% for those aged 25 to 34.

Underemployment within the same quarter rose slightly amongst the 25 to 34 age group from 22.2% in Q2 2017 to 22.3% in Q3 2017; and declined slightly amongst the 15 to 24 age group from 35.1% in Q2 2017 to 34.2% in Q3 2017.

As of Q3 2017, 67.3% of young people aged 15-24 years were either underemployed (engaged in work for less than 20 hours a week or low skilled work not commensurate with their skills and qualifications) or unemployed (have no work at all but willing and actively seeking to work), compared to 64.6% in the previous quarter.

The combined underemployment plus unemployment rate for the 25 to 34-year age group stood at 42.5% within the quarter under review, compared with 39.6% in the previous quarter.

Combined unemployment and underemployment rate for the entire youth labor force (15-35 years) was 52.65% or 22.64 million (10.96 million unemployed and another 11.68 million underemployed), compared to 45.65% in Q3 2016, 47.41% in Q4 2016 and 49.70% in Q3 2017. Unemployment tends to be higher for people within the labor force that have post-secondary school (31.8% unemployment rate and 50.0% combined unemployment and underemployment in Q3 2017).

Graduates tend to prefer fewer-in-supply white collar jobs rather than often rural, seasonal and low skilled and lower paying blue-collar jobs that are more in supply.

Unemployment and underemployment rates vary according to the nature of economic activity predominant in each state. States with higher focus on seasonal agriculture tend to have higher rates of underemployment compared to unemployment and may swing from high fulltime employment during periods of planting and harvest when they are fully engaged on their farms to periods of underemployment and even unemployment at other periods in between.

States with higher propensity of women to marry early or be housewives and hence will not be considered part of the labor force also tend to have lower unemployment rates. These states tend to have higher proportion of their economically active populations outside the labor force thereby reducing the number looking for work and hence the number that can be unemployed. While inter-state unemployment and underemployment rates to determine performance is not advised due to the effect on migration on any states level at any point (people can move from one state to another in search of employment thereby increasing the rate in the destination state and reducing the rate in the state they left from), nevertheless, in Q3 2017, Rivers State reported the highest unemployment rate (41.82%)followed by Akwa-Ibom (36.58%), Bayelsa state (30.36%), and Imo state (29.47%) while Katsina, Jigawa, Gombe, and Yobe, recorded the highest underemployment rates during the reviewing period, of 46.19%, 43.01%, 38.38%, and respectively.

Source: National Bureau of Statistics (Open Data)

Corruption Hegemony

The statistics and economic indices are depressing enough and certainly do not give much to cheer about, even though it is a sad commentary that a nation with such significant potentials still wallows in steep poverty. Agreed, a complexity of factors is culpable for the state of things.

However, there is one vice that voraciously seeks to swallow the whole nation alive. It is no news to the ordinary Nigerian that corruption is the pride of its leaders. Public funds to the tunes of trillions of Naira and dollars are fond of disappearing from government coffers. Public officials make pilfering, siphoning, racketeering, misappropriation, sharp practices and mismanagement of public funds their stock in trade. The group's most popular umbrella name? Corruption.

The led are not immune either. From the office assistant, who feels he is entitled to a tip before he can fetch an official file from the next office, to the traders, who are out to make inordinate gains from their customers, corruption seems to be part of the very air Nigerians breathe.

For a country once prided as the giant of Africa, it is unbelievably distressing that one which ought to be a vanguard for outstanding accomplishments is many at times caught at the forefront of international disrepute and embarrassment. Unfortunately, the trend, the hegemony of corruption, which has been a jarring assault on any prevalent form of sensibility or morality, seems to be increasing by the day, even when government portends to fight corruption. Without sugar-coating, the magnanimity of reported cases of corruption perpetrated by government officials, politicians and leaders across board is to say the least, mind-boggling and makes one readily cover his or her face in shame. These incidents have conveniently succeeded in eroding the belief and confidence of many. Take some corruption cases (abridged) below as compiled by Terkula Igidi of *Daily Trust* published on January 1, 2017:

1.   Dame Patience Jonathan ($15.5million scandal)
While investigating a former Special Adviser to ex-president Goodluck Jonathan on Domestic Affairs, Waripamowei Dudafa, the Economic and Financial Crimes Commission (EFCC) had stumbled on four company bank accounts in Skye Bank. The companies are Pluto Property and Investment Company Limited; Seagate Property Development and Investment Company Limited; Trans Ocean Property & Investment Company Limited; and Globus Integrated Service Limited. The joint balance of the four accounts, as of the time it was frozen, was said to be $15, 591,700.

The EFCC had invited the DSS officials, who during the former president's term in office, had been attached to the immediate past First Lady, to explain their roles in the scandal. The commission had evidence that these officials had, on several occasions, deposited money into certain accounts in Skye Bank, between 2013 and 2015.
However, the former First Lady has not been invited by the anti-graft agency even after she had laid claim to the huge sum of money. Instead, she has taken EFCC to court for daring to investigate her. The former First Lady accused the EFCC of hiring mercenaries as directors of the company in an attempt to rob her of her hard-earned money.
The four companies, standing trial before a Federal High Court in Lagos, have since pleaded guilty to money laundering.

Patience, who has sued Skye Bank for N200m, also has another account under the name 'Patience Ibifaka Jonathan' in the bank, which had a balance of $5m. That account was, however, not frozen by the commission.

2. Sambo Dasuki: The former National Security Adviser's $2.1 billion corruption case may be mind boggling but it looks like it will linger for a while.
Dasuki was thrown into jail since December 2015 and even though he has been granted bail by court, the Federal Government has refused to comply. He remains incarcerated while his case, alongside others. *His case came up in court on January 25, 2017 in an Abuja High Court.

3. The Economic and Financial Crimes Commission (EFCC) had probed a former Minister of Petroleum, Mrs. Diezani Allison-Madueke over misappropriation of $10 billion slush fund, in which her property assets in Abuja worth N4billion were frozen while the EFCC is also facilitating the freezing of her assets in Port Harcourt worth N3 billion.
The anti-graft agency has also frozen Diezani's foreign bank accounts in the United Kingdom and in Switzerland while the Federal Government through the Attorney-General of the Federation is working to freeze her United States property.
Despite all these, she is yet to be arraigned in court. However, Jide Omokore, a business associate of Diezani's is currently on bail after the EFCC arrested and charged him over fraud.

4. The Economic and Financial Crimes Commission (EFCC) had arraigned in absentia, a former Niger Delta militant leader, Government Ekpemupolo (alias Tompolo) before a Federal High Court in Lagos.
Early in 2016, the militant was arraigned alongside six brothers of a former Director-General of the Nigerian Maritime Administration and Safety Agency (NIMASA), Patrick Akpobolokemi.
They were arraigned on a 22-count charge, bordering on N47 billion fraud.
His accomplice, Patrick Akpobolokemi was arraigned alongside three others, Josephine Otuaga, Rita Uruakpa and Kime Engozu.
In the interim, the EFCC has frozen some of his identified assets.

5. A former governor of Adamawa State, Alhaji Murtala Nyako and his son, Abdulraziz Nyako, now a senator representing Adamawa Central on the platform of APC, were re-arraigned on N29 billion money laundering trial in September 2017.
The charges against the defendants include criminal conspiracy, abuse of office, opening of multiple bank accounts, and stealing to the tune of N29 billion.
The defendants, who were arraigned by the Economic and Financial Crimes Commission (EFCC), allegedly opened over 30 different accounts with Zenith Bank Plc. with the money between 2011 and 2013.

6. A former Chief of Defence Staff, Air Chief Marshal Alex Badeh (rtd.) has been charged with N3.9 billion case of corruption. Badeh was granted N2 billion bail.
The Economic and Financial Crimes Commission had said it traced 17 accounts to former Air Chief Marshal Alex Badeh (rtd).

Badeh was in January arrested for the non-specification of procurement costs, absence of contract agreements, award of contracts beyond authorised thresholds, transfer of public funds for unidentified purposes and general non-adherence to provisions of the Public Procurement Act.

7. Oliseh Metuh, a former spokesman of the People's Democratic Party (PDP) has been charged in 2 different cases.
First, he was charged with money laundering to the tune of N400 Million for which he was granted N400 bail.
He was also charged with criminal destruction of evidence but granted bail of N300 million. Metuh however, appealed for his case to be dismissed. The Appeal court ruled against him, stating that he has a case to answer.

8. The EFCC has also charged a former minister, under ex-president Olusegun Obasanjo, Femi Fani-Kayode and others with N4.9 billion fraud. He was however granted N250 million bail. The former PDP chieftain sued the Federal Government over his two months' detention by the EFCC but Justice Adeniyi ruled against him stating that the EFCC was acting within its statutory mandate.

9. Senate President, Bukola Saraki's false assets declaration trial seems to linger on endlessly. In April 2017, a Federal High Court in Abuja dismissed his application to stop the trial at the Code of Conduct Tribunal in Abuja. The Supreme Court had also dismissed Saraki's application challenging the jurisdiction of the tribunal to try him.

10. The arrest of judges over corruption allegations appeared to be the climax of the fight against corruption. On October 8, the Department of State Services (DSS) raided homes of some senior judges across the country. Justices Sylvester Ngwuta and John I. Okoro of the Supreme Court were arrested. Also arrested in the sting operation were Justices Adeniyi Ademola and Nnamdi Dimgba of the Federal High Court, Abuja and Justice Mua'azu Pindiga of the High Court, Gombe. Justices Ngwuta and Ademola have so far been arraigned over charges of judicial misconduct, money laundering, illegal possession of multiple travel passports and firearms. They have pleaded not guilty to the charges and were granted bail.

Hope against Hope

Nigerians are a very hopeful lot. With enough of it in under our belt, we might actually someday get to witness a live sentencing of corrupt officials, whose actions and inactions have perpetually held the nation's progress by the jugular.

Enough of the lip service being paid to the fight against corruption by government which has derided us and made us a laughing stock amongst nations! A deluded people can head nowhere, hope or no hope.

Chapter 6

Lessons from Singapore

An analysis of past challenges and subsequent successes of other nations might serve as an impetus to spur us on the right track. Singapore readily comes to mind.
The following narrative is derived from the eighth edition of Singapore's Recent Economic and Political Developments Yearbook.

Early History

The island of Singapore was known to mariners, at least by the third century A.D. By the seventh century, when a succession of maritime states arose throughout the Malay Archipelago, Singapore probably was one of the many trading outposts serving as an entrepôt and supply point for Malay, Thai, Javanese, Chinese, Indian, and Arab traders. A fourteenth-century Javanese chronicle referred to the island as Temasek, and seventeenth-century Malay annals noted the 1299 founding of the city of Singapura ("lion city") after a strange, lion-like beast that had been sighted there. Singapura was controlled by a succession of regional empires and Malayan sultanates.

When the Europeans were to invade the territory, it was the Portuguese, who first raised their flag there. Portuguese explorers captured the port of Melaka (Malacca) in 1511, forcing the reigning sultan to flee south, where he established a new regime, the Johore Sultanate that incorporated Singapura. The Portuguese burned down a trading post at the mouth of the Temasek River in 1613; after that, the island was largely abandoned and trading and planting activities moved south to the Riau Islands and Sumatra. However, planting activities had returned to Temasek by the early nineteenth century. In 1818, Temasek was settled by a Malay official of the Johore Sultanate and his followers, who shared the island with several hundred indigenous tribal people and Chinese planters.

The year 1819 marked the arrival of Sir Thomas Stamford Raffles, the lieutenant governor of the British enclave of Bencoolen (Bengkulu on the west coast of Sumatra) and an agent of the British East India Company, who obtained permission from the local Malay official to establish a trading post. He called it Singapore, after its ancient name, and opened the port to free trade and free immigration on the south coast of the island at the mouth of the Singapore River. At the time, Singapore had about 1,000 inhabitants. By 1827, the Chinese had become the most numerous of Singapore's various ethnic groups. They came from Malacca, Penang, Riau, and other parts of the Malay Archipelago. More recent Chinese migrants came from the South China provinces of Guangdong and Fujian.

During the 50 years following Raffles' establishment of his free-trade port, Singapore grew in size, population, and prosperity. In 1824, the Dutch formally recognized British control of Singapore, and London acquired full sovereignty over the island. From 1826 to 1867, Singapore, along with two other trading ports on the Malay Peninsula— Penang and Malacca—and several smaller dependencies, were ruled together as the Straits Settlements from the British East India Company headquarters in India. In 1867 the British needed a better location than fever-ridden Hong Kong to station their troops in Asia, so the Straits Settlements were made a crown colony and its capital Penang, was ruled directly from London. The British installed a governor as well as executive and legislative councils. By that time, Singapore had surpassed the other Straits Settlements in importance, as it had grown to become a bustling seaport with 86,000 inhabitants. Singapore also dominated the Straits Settlements Legislative Council. After the Suez Canal opened in 1869 and steamships became the major form of ocean transport, British influence increased in the region, bringing still greater maritime activity to Singapore. Later in the century and into the twentieth century, Singapore became a major point of disembarkation for hundreds of thousands of laborers brought in from China, India, the Dutch East Indies and the Malay Archipelago, bound for tin mines and rubber plantations to the north.

During the first half of the twentieth century, Singapore prospered, as financial institutions, transportation, communications, and government infrastructure expanded rapidly to support the booming trade and industry of the British Empire. Although Singapore was largely unaffected by World War I (1914–18), still it experienced the same postwar depression as the rest of the world. Along with the influx of Chinese migrants over the previous decades, came secret societies and kinship and place-name associations that grew to have great influence on society. Political activities surfaced in Singapore among the large Chinese population, first in the early 1900s between advocates of the reform and revolution in China. Then, in the 1930s there was increased interest in developments in China, and many supported either the Chinese Communist Party or the Chinese Nationalist Party (Guomindang). The Malayan Communist Party (MCP) was established in 1930 and competed with local branches of the Guomindang. Both sides, however, strongly supported China against the rising tide of Japanese aggression. Some years earlier, in 1923, in reaction to Japan's increasing naval power, the British began building a large naval base at Singapore. It was costly and unpopular, but when completed in 1941, this "Gibraltar of the East" posed an attractive target for Japan.

In December 1941, Japan attacked Malaya, and by February 1942 the Japanese had taken control of both Malaya and Singapore. They renamed Singapore Shōnan ("Light of the South") and set about dismantling the British establishment. Singapore suffered greatly during this war, first from the Japanese attack and then from allied bombings of its harbor facilities. By the war's end, the colony was in poor shape, with a high death rate, rampant crime and corruption, and severe infrastructure damage. During the 1942–45 occupation, a favorable view of the colonial relationship had lapsed among the local population, as it had in other British colonies, and resulted in demands for self-rule upon the return of the British.

In 1946, Singapore became a separate crown colony with a civil administration. When the Federation of Malaya was established in 1948 as a move toward self-rule, Singapore continued as a separate crown colony. The same year, the MCP launched an insurrection in Malaya and Singapore, and the British declared a State of Emergency that was to continue until 1960. By this time, the worldwide demand for tin and rubber had brought economic recovery to Singapore and the Korean War (1950–53) brought even further economic prosperity to the colony. However, strikes and student demonstrations organized by the MCP throughout the 1950s continued to arouse fears of a communist takeover in Malaya.

In 1953, a British commission recommended partial internal self-government for Singapore. In this milieu, other political parties began to form in 1954. One was the Labour Front led by David Marshall, who called for immediate independence and merger with Malaya. The same year, the People's Action Party (PAP) was established under the leadership of Lee Kuan Yew, a Cambridge-educated lawyer. The PAP also campaigned for an end to colonialism and a merger with Malaya. Following Legislative Assembly elections in 1955, a coalition government was formed with Marshall as chief minister. As a result of further talks with London, Singapore was granted internal self-government while the British continued to control defense and foreign affairs. In 1957, Malaya was granted independence and the next year, the British Parliament elevated the status of Singapore from colony to state and provided for new local elections.

The PAP swept the elections held in May 1959, and Lee Kuan Yew was installed as the first prime minister. The PAP's strongest opponents were communists operating in both legal and illegal organizations. The most prominent was the Barisan Sosialis (Socialist Front), a left-wing party that retained favor in the 1960s and early 1970s. There also were fears that communists within the PAP would seize control of the government, but moderates led by Lee held sway. In 1962, Singaporean voters approved the PAP's merger plan with Malaya and on September 16, 1963, Singapore joined Malaya and the former British territories on the island of Borneo — Sabah and Sarawak — to form the independent Federation of Malaysia. Only Brunei opted out of the federation.

Singapore as Part of Malaysia
Between 1963 and 1965, Singapore was an integral part of the Federation of Malaysia. Union with Malaya had always been a goal of Lee Kuan Yew and the moderate wing of the PAP. Once the PAP ranks were firmly under Lee's control, he met with the leaders of Malaya, Sabah, and Sarawak to sign the Malaysia Agreement on July 9, 1963, under which the independent nation of

Malaysia was formed. Lee declared Singapore's independence from Britain on August 31, 1963; dissolved the Legislative Assembly; and called for an election to obtain a new mandate for the PAP pro-merger government. Many political opponents of the merger were jailed, and the PAP won a majority of seats in the assembly. Despite threats of military confrontation (Konfrontasi) from Indonesia and actual raids on Sabah and Sarawak by Indonesian commandos, the merger took place on September 16, 1963. The new federation was based on an uneasy alliance between Malays and ethnic Chinese. Communal rioting ensued in various parts of the new nation, including usually well-controlled Singapore. In the end, the merger failed. As a state, Singapore did not achieve the economic progress it had hoped for, and political tensions escalated between Chinese-dominated Singapore and Malay-dominated Kuala Lumpur, the capital of Malaysia. Fearing greater Singaporean dominance of the federation and further violence between the Muslim and Chinese communities, the government of Malaysia decided to separate Singapore from the fledgling federation.

Independent Singapore

After separation from Malaysia on August 9, 1965, Singapore was forced to accept the challenge of forging a viable nation—the Republic of Singapore—on a small island with few resources beyond the determination and talent of its people. Under the leadership of Lee Kuan Yew and the PAP, the new nation met the challenge. Konfrontasi with Indonesia ended in 1966, while trade with Japan and the United States increased substantially, especially with the latter, since Singapore became a supply center for the increasing U.S. involvement in the Second Indochina War (1954–75). In 1967 Singapore joined Brunei, Indonesia, Malaysia, the Philippines, and Thailand in forming the Association of Southeast Asian Nations (ASEAN) for the purpose of promoting regional stability, economic development, and cultural exchange. In 1968, Britain announced its decision to withdraw from its military bases in Singapore within three years. Because of defense implications and the amount of British spending (accounting for about 25 percent of the gross national product [GNP] of Singapore), this was sobering news. The government called for new elections, seeking a new mandate to proceed. Because the PAP won all 58 parliamentary seats, the government was able to pass stricter labor legislation and thus help overcome the nation's reputation for frequent labor disputes and strikes. Former British naval base workers were retrained to work in what became the Sembawang Shipyard, and eventually a major shipbuilding and ship repair center. By the 1970s, Singapore had achieved status as a world leader in shipping, air transport, and oil refining. No longer was Singapore as dependent on peninsular Malaysia for its economic prosperity.

Economic Success and Political Supremacy

In the 1970s through the 1990s, Singapore experienced sustained economic growth. Along with Hong Kong, South Korea, and Taiwan, it was called one of the "Four Tigers" of Asian economic prosperity. Labor-intensive industries were relocated to other ASEAN nations and were replaced by high-technology industries and services.

Note that the PAP developed a stable and corruption-free government, marked by strong central development planning and social policies. Despite paternalistic, and at times, authoritarian governmental practices and one-party dominance, the PAP maintained its large popular mandate. A Singaporean identity, distinct from that of the Malay and Chinese, emerged as the nation increasingly integrated itself into the global economy. In 1990, Lee Kuan Yew stepped down as prime minister, and Goh Chok Tong, the first deputy prime minister and first Minister of Defence, took over as part of the succession to a new generation of leaders.

The Asian economic crisis of 1997–98 was not a major setback for Singapore as it was for other Southeast Asian nations; the regional economic downturn did bring fluctuating growth rates to Singapore but posed no serious problems to it. Except for oil-rich Brunei, Singapore remains the most prosperous nation in the entire region. After 14 years in office, in 2004, Goh stepped down in favor of Lee Hsien Loong, the Minister of Finance, and son of Lee Kuan Yew. The elder Lee agreed to stay on as minister mentor and Goh, as senior minister in order to oversee the transition of the new generation of leaders. Lee Hsien Loong was confirmed into office via a democratic election held on May 6, 2006.

Nigeria, where art thou? Learning from a Success

Many economists the world over have been intrigued at the miracle called Singapore -from its devastated and almost nonentity state in the mid-1960s to becoming one of the top ten world economies in the 21st Century. The economic model of Singapore is certainly something Nigeria can and should learn from but as things stand, clandestine vices, coupled with blatant disregard for national advancement through dearth of visionary leadership, greed, tribalism, lack of patriotism, absence of coherent national direction, corruption and materialism; and religious fanaticism keep Nigeria away from the throes of economic emancipation, political stability and overall national progress.

Now, like never before, we need to be selfless because it is the only route to truly build a nation worth emulating, it is the only path to being the giant, the exemplary protagonist of potentials-turned-practicalities.
Nigeria has all the prospects and trappings of doing a transformational turnaround in 20 years, if only we imbibe fiscal discipline, build appropriate infrastructure, boost trade, open up the economy, shun corruption and entrench accountability in all spheres of national life.

In the next and final chapter, we will be looking at how to practically get our hands dirty, with the soil of hard-and-smart work, and thrust the nation's engine forward.

Chapter 7

Way Forward

Much has been said in the previous chapters. From how Nigeria came into existence, the infrastructural, economic and political upheavals the nation has had to grapple with through the decades (and still is grappling with), to Singapore's formidable success which Nigerians can roleplay to bring the Nigerian ship to the shores of our desired Eldorado.

In light of the foregoing, I have put forward some cogent, practicable steps which if followed through with firm political will, can bring the slumbering giant to the awakening of glorious achievements, international prestige, moral rectitude and acclaimed renown. As I mentioned in my introduction, these steps are not new. They have been mentioned at several fora and indeed, only political will put to work can make the required difference.

CONSTITUTIONAL REVIEW

The Lyttleton Constitution of 1954 was the fore runner to the 1979 Constitution as amended in 1999.
The 1954 Constitution, among others, made regional governments independent of the central government in respect of subjects and legislative powers allocated to them. It also established a unicameral legislature for the federal government and each of the 3 regional governments. In addition, Lagos was taken out of the control of any regional government and made the Federal Capital Territory; regional public services were established for each of the 3 regions; the judiciary was reorganized so as to establish regional judiciaries while autonomy was granted to the Southern Cameroons which was up till that time, part of a larger Nigeria and Northern Cameroons. Specifically, for the first time, ministers were given specific portfolios.
Thus, the Lyttleton Constitution could best be described as the transition instrument towards Nigeria's independence in 1960, under a federal structure with democratically elected federal and regional legislature.

Contrasting the Lyletton Constitution with the present (1999) Constitution - To do this effectively, it is necessary to x-ray the 1979 Constitution. The 1979 Constitution set up Nigeria under a presidential system of government with a federal government, 19 state governments, a Federal Capital Territory, 3 arms and 3 levels of government. Like the 1963 Constitution, the life-span of the 1979 constitution was abruptly terminated on 31st December, 1983 when the civilian administration of President Shehu Shagari and Vice President Alex Ekwueme was toppled and replaced by the military dictatorship of Generals Muhammed Buhari and Tunde Idiagbon. That regime seeded 3 other extra-constitutional regimes – the General Ibrahim Babangida military dictatorship (1985-1993), Mr. Ernest Shonekan interim civilian-led regime, General Sani Abacha military dictatorship (1993-1998) and General Abdulsalami Abubakar military administration which successfully ushered in the 3rd Republic on the 27th of May, 1999 with the introduction of the 1999 Constitution.

The 1999 constitution catered to the dynamics of the current reality of democracy with 36 states and 774 local government areas. This was significant as it was the standard for our democracy to follow three arms and levels of government, with Abuja as the Federal Capital Territory.
Close inspection shows that the Lyttleton Constitution was the bridge to our current constitution, differing only in shape and context. While the former was a regional and parliamentary system, the latter (our present) embraces the presidential system.

I am of the firm opinion that while (for a plethora of reasons) it might be impossible to return to the regional form of government, legacy makes a demand of us to review the present constitution in line with our current realities. Nothing is cast in stone. As I insist, what is first and foremost required is the political will to effect the amendment and needed modification.
The constitutional review has been a loud clamour in recent times, and it is time to do the needful.

POWER

There is no need to mollycoddle the state of affairs - in order to tackle the epileptic power supply that has virtually crippled the Nigerian economy, drastic draconian steps have to be taken.

a. Decentralization of the Power Grid
The power needs for over 180 million people is massive. And much so, when you realize that over 40 per cent of this teeming population are vibrant youth, ready for commercial, manufacturing and productive activities. Presently, the national grid is oversaturated and overburdened. It is vital that we decentralize the grid system. There is need to have multiple grids, and several substations generating power apart from the national grid as we have it now.

b. Alternate Sources
The world never rests on its oars – the dynamics are ever changing. The world over, countries are constantly seeking for alternate sources of power, which are primarily cheaper, cleaner, environment-friendly and more efficient in the long-run. Nigeria cannot

afford to be left behind. We must look to alternate sources of power generation besides hydro and gas.
Investments in wind and nuclear will undoubtedly serve us judiciously. For the industrial development we envisage for Nigeria, having multiple sources of energy and power is not just a good idea. It is a compulsion.

A while ago, I was in Somerset to see the ongoing work at the nuclear power plant in Hinckley. Hinckley Point C nuclear power station (HPC) is a project to construct a 3,200 MWe nuclear power station with two EPR (nuclear reactors) in Somerset, England. This project is jointly funded by EDF of France and CGN of China and would cost a whooping £20.3 billion.
In the light of giant strides such as this, Nigeria cannot shy away from exploring other sources if she is to meet her power needs sufficiently and still have excess.

   c. Revisit the Power Reform Act 2005

The Electric Power Sector Reform Act of 2005 was aimed at creating a new legal and regulatory framework for the power sector. It was what set the stage for NEPA's disbandment and led to the privatization process; amongst other things, a Consumer assistance fund to bridge the funding gaps for low income earners is part of what the Act covers.

As laudable and beautiful as the Power Reform Act is, it might be calling for a revision in tandem with current realities. It is crystal clear that the power distribution companies are in disarray due to various challenges, chief amongst which is funding. There are also many issues bordering on licensing and reinvestment that should be looked into. Additionally, and quite importantly, the power sector is in need of greater liberalization, though admittedly, that ought to be a steady work-in-progress.

INFRASTRUCTURE UPGRADE

Nigerian road networks are on the whole, quite sporadic, alternating between good, fair and poor across the country. Nigeria still has a long way to go. There is pressing, urgent need to improve existing infrastructure -most of which are decrepit and moribund, and thus increasingly less competitive. The quicker we attend to these, the better for all. Luckily, all hope is not lost, as a multi-pronged approach can help achieve this laudable feat viz:

   a. Increased Spending

For Nigeria to be able to compete favorably with the larger economies of the world, more funds need to be earmarked for road and infrastructure development. It has to be stated that infrastructure spending would greatly boost the GDP of Nigeria to a percentile of over 20%. Currently, the N558 billion budgeted for infrastructure this year (2018) is not sufficient to reverse the many years of decadence and open up the economy. Government should be open to private sector funding in infrastructural development, if it is unable to provide adequate funding.

Additionally, there is need to have a year-on-year infrastructure quantum leap, if we are to become economic giants. It would interest anyone to know that China has a consistent spend of over 5 trillion dollars on their belt and road initiative. The area of the initiative is primarily Asia and Europe, encompassing approximately 60 countries, including Oceania and East Africa. Anticipated cumulative investment over an indefinite timescale is variously put at US$4 trillion or US$8 trillion.

This singular initiative has been contrasted with the two US-centric trading arrangements, the Trans-Pacific Partnership and the Transatlantic Trade and Investment Partnership. A prime example of the network is the Silk Road Railway debuted in 2013, which goes through China's Xinjiang Autonomous Region, Kazakhstan, Russia, Belarus, Poland and Germany as a land connection between Asia and Europe.

b. Skills transfer mechanism
One of the pertinent challenges troubling and weighing Nigeria badly is skills gaps. The artisanal skills gap is so mammoth that Nigerians still depend on Beninois to fix floor tiles in our building and construction sites. For infrastructural resurgence, we must have skills transfer and skills development hubs. We need to also reawaken our technical colleges and hold them to task. Singapore achieved its feats by creating education quotas in tandem with growth prospects and outlook. We must identify the skills gap on road and rail construction, and develop competencies around these areas to ensure growth and development. It is shameful that our current infrastructure is in the league of the American standards of the 1970s.

c. Strategic fiscal discipline and project management
Many government projects are grounded ever before they take off due to insincerity on the part of government contractors, who are fond of abandoning projects halfway even after collecting full payment on same. We must develop fiscal discipline in project execution. Over N20 billion has gone down the drain in the last five years due to corruption in project execution processes and the constant delays in project execution becomes sickening. The Mambila Plateau has been noted for its huge potential in the power sector and nothing has been done about it until now. It took 10 years to complete Lagos/Ibadan Expressway, Shagamu/Benin and other roads that are supposed to provide linkages to boost trade and investment have been disrupted. Nigeria needs to be critical in approach to these issues.

d. Unburdening the Roads

Much like the power sector, it is pertinent that we seek alternate ways to unburden the roads from the overbearing weight of human and goods cargo. If we looked in various directions, the wear and tear on the roads will drastically reduce, leading to longer shelf life and low accident rates, amongst other myriad socio-economic benefits.

Therefore, it is imperative to seek expansion on monorail networks. I believe strongly that effective monorail networks should be implemented in Nigeria based on the growth projections and the population dispensation for the next 30 years, which is about twice our present statistics. Considering this projection, nothing short of a mass transit system will work satisfactorily for the Nigerian population.

Luckily again, Nigeria is blessed with copious waterways of lagoons, and rivers. As a matter of fact, there is barely any Nigerian state without a major river flowing within it. We should therefore think of effectively enhancing our inland waterways to harness its great potentials and relieve the roads substantially.
In the words of a foremost maritime industry participant "Stakeholders in the water transportation sector had at different fora harped on the need for big companies such as the Dangote Group to embrace the alternative of transporting their products through the waterways instead of hauling them via the roads.....Water transport is indeed the most sustainable mode of transportation for the future. Nigeria can make good use of the waterways in various ways because the maritime industry is very large such that we have so many vessels coming in. However, one of the things I noticed on our waterways is that there are wrecks in the water and that has caused many ships not to come in. Though, the Nigerian Ports Authority (NPA), Nigerian Maritime Administration and Safety Agency (NIMASA) and other government agencies are trying to remove all the wrecks. The waterways are big and so it can create jobs for many people." (www.shipsandports.com.ng)

INDUSTRY

Economic Policy Review and Consolidation of Vision 20:20

In an earlier chapter, mention was made of the three earliest industrial plans several governments attempted to put in place, since independence, in the bid to industrialize the nation. To ensure industrial stability and development, it is paramount to have continuous economic policy reviews. In addition, all existing policies ought to be harmonized.

Presently, the economic transformation agenda, otherwise known as Nigeria Vision 20:20, sets the direction for the industrial policy in Nigeria. The industrialization strategy aims at achieving greater global competitiveness in the production of specific processed and manufactured goods by effectively linking industrial activity with primary sector activity, domestic and foreign trade, and service activity.
Towards this end, the strategy includes the following objectives:

- Stimulate primary production to enhance the competitiveness of Nigeria's real sector;
- Significantly increase the production of processed and manufactured goods for export;
- Stimulate domestic and foreign trade in value added goods and services;

• Strengthen linkages among key sectors of the economy.

On the basis of the above objectives, the country is pursuing and promoting a comprehensive policy of cluster development in the manufacturing and processing industries. Through private-public partnerships, the strategy will promote efficient and intensive mechanisms for the processing and manufacturing of select export materials.
In pursuance of the above policy strategy, the economic transformation agenda highlights a number of issues to be addressed. These include the development of industrial parks, industrial clusters, enterprise zones and incubator facilities.

The industrial parks which will be created for large manufacturing companies to ensure high value addition in the production of finished products or raw materials is expected to cover areas not less than 3,050km2. The parks will be created, based on geographical zones to focus on the development of resources in which each zone has comparative and competitive advantage. Hence, the following business activities have been identified for each of the zones (NPC 2009).

• North east: agriculture and solid minerals e.g. gypsum, biomass, ethanol, biodiesel, tropical fruits, etc.
• North west: gum arabic, livestock and meat processing, tanneries, bio fuel etc.
• North central; fruit processing, cotton, quarries, furniture and minerals; boards. plastic processing, leather goods, garments etc.
• South east: palm oil refining and palm tree processing into biomass particle boards, plastic processing, leather goods and garments
• South west: manufacturing (especially garments, methanol, etc.), distributive trade, general goods, plastic etc., and;
• South south: petrochemicals, manufacturing (plastic, fertilizer, and fabrications, etc.), oil services and distributive trade (Tinapa)

The industrial clusters which will be established with the participation and assistance of states and local governments will form oases of industrial activities and commerce, and will cover areas of between 100 and 1,000 hectares. The location of the clusters will take into cognizance access to roads, railways, sea ports, cargo airports, and proximity to a city and management will be through a private cluster company.
Meanwhile, private investors, or property developers, could also establish and run industrial clusters in each state. Nevertheless, industrial incentives similar to those in industrial parks will also be provided while each cluster will have a skill acquisition/training centre for SME's providing different modules.

The Enterprise zones are platforms of 5-30 hectares, targeted at incorporating the informal sector into the organized private sector. This will empower farmers and small and medium-scale enterprises and enable them to efficiently and conveniently feed their products into the value-chain of large-scale industries. They will be located in both state capitals and local government areas. These centres will accommodate mechanics, block makers, small-scale furniture manufacturers, timber merchants, welders/metal fabricators, garment makers, and other categories of artisans and vocational workers who constitute over 70 per cent of Nigeria's private sector. Skills acquisition/training centres will also be located in each enterprise zone for skills upgrading, while management of the enterprise zones will be handled by the private sector. The incubators will be start-up centres for new and inexperienced entrepreneurs, graduates of tertiary institutions, investors and vocational persons wishing to set up their own businesses. In these centres, prospective start-ups will be equipped with entrepreneurial skills to help development.

Sectoral Incentives

It is worth noting that the Nigerian Government has put up a number of investment incentives, which according to the Nigerian Investment Promotion Commission, are for the stimulation of private sector investment from within and outside the country. While some of these incentives cover all sectors, other are limited to some specific sectors. The nature and application of these incentives have been considerably simplified.
Select sectoral incentives include:

Manufacturing
• Companies with turnover of less than NGN1 million are taxed at a low rate of 20 per cent for the first five years of operation if they are in the manufacturing sector;
• Dividends from companies in the manufacturing sector with a turnover of less than NGN1 million are tax-free for the first five years of operation;
• Dividends derived from manufacturing companies in the petrol chemical, and liquefied natural gas sub-sector are exempt from tax.

Agriculture and Agro-Industry
• Companies in the agro-allied business do not have their capital allowance restricted. It is granted in full i.e. 100 per cent;
• The payments of minimum tax by companies that make small or no profits at all do not apply to agro allied businesses;
Agro-allied plants and equipment enjoy enhanced capital allowances of up to 50 per cent;
• The processing of agricultural produce is a pioneer industry; consequently, there is a 100 per cent tax-free period for five years;
• All agricultural and agro-industrial machines and equipment are subject to only a 1 per cent duty;
• The agricultural credit guarantee scheme fund administered by the Central Bank of Nigeria: up to 75 per cent guarantee for all loans granted by commercial banks for agricultural production, and processing;
• Interest drawback programme fund: 60 per cent repayment of interest paid by those who borrow from banks under the ACGS, for the purpose of cassava production and processing provided such borrowers repay their loans on schedule.

Solid Minerals

• Three to five years tax holiday;
• Low income tax of between 20 and 30 per cent;
• Deferred royalty payments, depending on the magnitude of the investment and the strategic nature of the project;
• Possible capitalization of expenditure on exploration and surveys;
• Extension of infrastructure such as roads and electricity to mining sites;
• The holder of a mining lease shall, where qualified, be entitled to:

- o   Depreciation or capital allowance of 75 per cent of the certified true capital expenditure incurred in the year of investment and 50 per cent in subsequent years;
- o   Investment allowance of 5 per cent;
- o   Exemption from payment of customs and import duties;
- o   Expatriate quota and resident permit for approved expatriate personnel;
- o   In addition to roll-over relief under the capital gains tax, companies replacing their plants
and machinery are to enjoy a once-and-for-all 95 per cent capital allowance in the first
year, with 5 per cent retention value until the asset is disposed.

Private Sector Collaboration

Furthermore, to bring about global competitiveness in tandem with Vision 20:20 and beyond, efforts should be redoubled via collaborations with the private sector.

For much of the 1970s up to the early 1980s, there was little linkage between the public and
private sector. The late 1980s marked a shift in economic thinking, leading to greater reorganization of the pivotal role of the private sector in the process of development. This logically meant greater engagement in dialogue with the private sector on economic policy-making.
The private sector is organized around trade groups, under the umbrella of the Manufacturers Association of Nigeria (MAN) which is a national industrial association representing nearly 2000 companies in the private and public sectors. These companies are engaged in the manufacturing, construction, and service sectors of the economy. The association's role is advisory and consultative, but has also occasionally joined issues with government and other bodies on matters relating to industrial and broad economic policy.

Since its establishment in 1971, MAN has gradually positioned itself as a respected organization by the government. This has led to routine consultations between the Federal Government and the association to harvest input from them and factor interests of its membership into industrial policy even from the conception stage. MAN and the more general, organized private sector

(OPS) are often invited to serve on many committees set up by government and other local and
international organizations. It is not atypical to find forums where the government, the private
sector (MAN), and the donor community come together to discuss a series of diagnostic
assessments of Nigeria's business environment and forge an agenda for reform.

Business co-ordination efforts in Nigeria have been largely successful, although the fortunes of
the manufacturing sector remain abysmal, given its low share of GDP and recent spate of closure of firms. The exchanges between the government and the private sector are often cordial and robust. This has inspired a number of initiatives and interventions directed at improving performance in the sector, including the establishment of the Bank of Industry (BoI), and Small and Medium Industries Development Agency (SMEDAN), SMIEIS, etc.

Additionally, government has magnanimously in recent times provided intervention in critical sectors - NGN200 billion disbursed to about 518 companies across the country for the restructuring and refinancing of the manufacturing sector; NGN126 billion as export expansion grant; NGN100 billion textile sector bailout fund; NGN200 billion for small and medium industries guarantee scheme and NGN7.5 billion for national automotive fund, disbursed to 25 companies.
Seeing the fruits of these efforts, the onus lies on government, more public-private collaborations are imperative to fast-track development.

POLITICAL WILL AND STABILITY

The political stability of any form of government has to involve the unwavering realization of its political and governmental kernel. The political stability of a communal gerontocracy in villages and small towns headed by elders under an age grade system means the continuation of the exercise of power by those who have reached the appropriate age at various levels of the system. The political stability of a feudal monarchy means the continuation of the exercise of power by the heirs of the dynasty or dynasties, who produce the monarch.

It is a sad commentary that many of Nigeria's democratically elected officers, who swore solemnly on the Holy Koran or the Holy Bible to carry out their legislative and executive duties in accordance with the provisions of the constitution, carry on as if the Fundamental Objectives and Directive Principles contained therein do not exist. Or perhaps if they did, they are words merely intended to decorate a document, whose main usefulness is to keep the soldiers out, get the equally overzealous civilians into office and ceremoniously hand them the keys to the public treasury. This crooked rationale is the reason that ever before this democratic government took off, it was threatened with instability.

Instead of facing up to clear constitutional responsibilities, many elected officers employ all sorts of devices and gimmicks to evade their duties and position themselves to rule like dictators and monarchs, as though that is what they were elected for. This kind of attitude will get us nowhere.

The political stability of democracy, as provided for in our Constitution means the continuation of the exercise of power by those freely elected by the people of this country for specific periods with definite mandates, which conform to the Fundamental Objectives and Directive Principles of State Policy clearly defined in chapter II of the Constitution. The opening section of this second chapter in the Constitution makes is very explicit, providing that:

> 13.   It shall be the duty and responsibility of all organs of government and of all authorities and persons exercising legislative executive or judicial powers, to conform to, observe and apply the provisions of these chapters of the Constitution.
>
> 14(i) The Federal Republic of Nigeria shall be a state based on the principles of democracy and social justice.
>
> (2) If it is hereby accordingly declared that -
>
> (a) sovereignty belongs to the people of Nigeria from whom government through this Constitution derives all its powers and authority.
>
> (b) the security and welfare of the people shall be the primary purpose of government.

Invariably, the clause as stated in the Constitution points to us that the political stability of our democracy should not be confused with the stability of the power in the hands any individual elected into office, as some would want to sit-tight.

At the same time, the Nigerian populace is not to be held to ransom by the whims and caprices of elected officials and ruling class, who might choose to wrongly wield power through manipulation, gerrymandering and unnecessarily heating the polity to their own gain and the detriment of the masses. Resultant which, these supposed leaders become instruments of destruction instead of vanguards of national progress and harmony.

There can only be stability for our democracy, if those freely elected lead in accordance with the Fundamental Objectives and Directive Principles of State Policy and, as they make the security and welfare of the people the primary purpose of government and governance. The power bestowed on any elected official is at the end of it all, for the welfare and advancement of those who elected him or her into office.

In a Nutshell

In conclusion, as brilliant and good as these policies and suggestions are, they remain mere recommendations and political so long as the political will and doggedness are not set in motion to wrestle the issues of infrastructural decadence, corruption, retrogressive fiscal policies, and other socio-economic depravities that presently serve as stumbling blocks on the road to progress.

A stitch in time saves nine!

God bless Nigeria!

REFERENCES

NAI. CSO 1/1/13, Denton to Knutsford, 8 June 1891. It should be noted that one pound sterling (£) was equivalent to 20 shillings(s), each of which was equal to 12 pence (d)

NAI, CSO 1/1/14. Denton to Ripon, 11 October 1893.

NAI. CSO 1/1/14, Carter to Ripon 11 December 1893.

NAI, CSO 1/1/22, Gov., Lagos, to Chamberlain. 30 June 1897.

NAI. CSO 1/1/22, Governor. Lagos to Chamberlain. 23 July 1897. enc. for report on mistakes by DPW and two others, dated 20 July 1897.

CSO 1/1/23, Denton to Chamberlain, 29 August 1898.

NAI, Comcol 1 1532, "Street Lighting in Lagos," W. Taylor to Comcol, 26 November 1943.

NAI, Comcol 1 1532, L.G. Purkis, Assistant Superintendent of Police to Supt. of Police, 17 December, 1943.

NAI, Comcol 1 1532, Comcol to Fin. Sec. Lagos, 26 August 1944.

National Electric Power Authority (NEPA) Ijora Power Station (Brochure), 1998, pp. 2-4

NAI, Comcol 1 2823, "Ijora Power Station," Director of Public Works (DPW) to Director of Marine, 4 March 1943.

Nigerian Pioneer (Lagos). 25 February 1927, Random Notes & News

NAI, Comcol 1 1424, "Lagos Electricity Supply-Bad Debts," The Accountant, Electric Light Accounts Branch, Public Works Department (PWD), Lagos to Chief Accountant, PWD, 4 January 1932.

Ibid.

NAI, Comcol 1 1424, Chief Secretary to the Government (CSG) to Comcol, 15 November 1933; CSG to Comcol, 8 December 1934.

NAI, Comcol 1 1424. Comcol to Treasurer. 8 December 1934.

NAI, Comcol 1 1424, DPW to Comcol, 3 October 1934.

NAI, Comcol 1 1532, Commissioner for Lands to CSG, 13 September 1932.

Books

Acemoglu, D. and Robinson, J. *Why Nations Fail: The Origins of Power, Prosperity, and Poverty*. Crown Business. March 20, 2012. Pg.43-4

Ademoyega, Adewale *On Why We Struck.* Evans Brothers (Ibadan, Nigeria). 1981.

Echeruo, M. *Victorian Lagos: Aspects of Nineteenth Century Lagos Life*. London: Macmillan. 1977, pp. 20-21.

Mills, Greg. *Why Africa is Poor, and what Africans can do about it*. Penguin Global. November 17, 2010

Moghalu, Kingsley Chiedu. *Emerging Africa: How the Global Economy's 'Last Frontier' Can Prosper and Matter.* Bookcraft Ltd. June 8th 2013.

Singapore Recent Economic and Political Developments Yearbook (5th edition). International Business Publications, USA, 2008, pp.1-5

Siollun, Max. *Soldiers of Fortune: A History of Nigeria (1983-1993)*. Cassava Republic Press. September 2nd 2013, pp.3,4.

Walker, Robin. *Intellectual Life and Legacy of Timbuktu*. Reklaw Education Lecture series Book 1.First published May 22nd, 2011.

Online sources

Aba Women Riot Receives UN Recognition - PM NEWS Nigeria
https://www.pmnewsnigeria.com › aba-w...

Between law and history: the Berlin Conference of 1884-1885 and the logic.
https://academic.oup.com › lril › article

Compilation on corruption. Ten corruption cases to watch in 2017By Terkula Igidi | Publish Date: Jan 1 2017 2:00AM. https://www.dailytrust.com.ng/news/feature/10-corruption-cases-to-watch
-in-2017/178565.html

How over N11tr for electricity was squandered under OBJ, Yar'Adua, Jonathan – SERAP Report ON AUGUST 9, 20173:42 PM.
https://www.vanguardngr.com/2017/08/n11tr-electricity-squandered-obj-yaradua-jonathan-
serap/

How Aba Women Riot split Igboland - Vanguard News
https://www.vanguardngr.com ›

http://www.naijanomics.com/2011/10/06/how-did-we-get-here-nigeria/

http://shipsandports.com.ng/can-nigeria-maximize-use-inland-waterways/ ISSUES IN THE NEWS. How can Nigeria maximize the use of its inland waterways?
Ships & Ports on August 7, 2017

https://en.wikipedia.org/wiki/Boko_Haram_insurgency

https://en.wikipedia.org/wiki/Economy_of_Nigeria (Economy of Nigeria)

Investment incentives on NIGERIAN INVESTMENT PROMOTION COMMISSION website
https://www.invest-nigeria.com/investment-incentives/

Idris Alooma: Warrior King of the Bornu Empire - Inside Arewa
http://insidearewa.com.ng/2017/08/06/idris-alooma-warrior-king-bornu-empire/

Learning to compete, working paper no.8. Industry development and growth in Nigeria: Lessons and challenges. by LN Chete et al sponsored by the Brookings Institution (cited for 1st, 2nd and 3rd Industry plans). Paper on https://www.brookings.edu/wp-content/uploads/2016/07/L2C_WP8_Chete-et-al-1.pdf

National Bureau of Statistics Source for Statistics on Employment rate.

Nigerian roads and connectivity. https://www.pwc.com/gx/en/transportation-logistics/publications/africa-infrastructure-investment/assets/nigeria.pdf, pg. 6

Olukoju, Ayodeji. *Infrastructure development and urban facilities in Lagos, 1861-2000*. http://books.openedition.org/ifra/829?lang=en

www.ingramcontent.com/pod-product-compliance
Lightning Source LLC
Chambersburg PA
CDIIW050050260726
48658CB00005B/1872